BIRDS

OF

VANCOUVER

AND THE LOWER MAINLAND

ROBIN BOVEY • WAYNE CAMPBELL
Illustrated by EWA PLUCIENNIK

LONE
PINE

The Publisher:
Lone Pine Publishing
#206 10426-81 Avenue
Edmonton, Alberta, Canada
T6E 1X5

Canadian Cataloguing in Publication Data

Bovey, Robin B. (Robin Bruce), 1947-
  Birds of Vancouver

  ISBN 0-919433-73-1

  1. Birds - British Columbia - Vancouver.
2. Bird watching - British Columbia - Vancouver.
I. Campbell, Wayne. II. Pluciennik, Ewa, 1954-
III. Ho, Kitty. IV. Title.
QL685.5.B7B69 1989 598.29711'33 C89-091089-8

Cover Design: Ewa Pluciennik
Colour Illustrations: Ewa Pluciennik, Kitty Ho & Joan Johnston
Black and White Illustrations: Donna McKinnon & Ewa Pluciennik
Book Design and Layout: Yuet Chan & Ewa Pluciennik
Typesetting: Michael Hawkins & Phillip Kennedy
Editorial: Mary Walters Riskin
Separations: Scangraphics Ltd.
Printing: Quality Color Press Inc.

Publisher's Acknowledgement
The publisher gratefully acknowledges the assistance of the Federal Department of Communications, Alberta Culture and Multiculturalism, the Canada Council, and the Alberta Foundation for the Literary Arts in the production of this book.

CONTENTS

PREFACE

Most of us have been intrigued by birds at one time or another. For some this interest has evolved into a pastime, but for most of us it is a small facet of our lives that we enjoy when we can.

Many people enjoy feeding birds and having them around the yard. Birdwatching provides us with a tangible contact with nature in an urban existence. This book is for people who enjoy birds, but who don't regard themselves as professional birdwatchers, people who would like to know more, without buying comprehensive field guides and expensive equipment and then trying to decide which birds are actually found in the urban environment. This is a guide for the back yard birdwatcher.

Each bird is illustrated in colour and there are descriptions and illustrations of the habitats within our city which are particularly attractive to birds. At the back of the book there is a section on how to attract birds to the yard. This section deals with feeders, nesting boxes and explains which trees, shrubs and garden settings are most attractive to birds.

ACKNOWLEDGEMENTS

The authors are grateful to the following for their advice, assistance and encouragement in the preparation of this book: Robert W. Butler, Eileen C. Campbell, Elizabeth John, Grant Kennedy and Kathie Kennedy.

The authors would also like to thank the Vancouver Natural History Society for their permission to use the *Checklist of Vancouver Birds*.

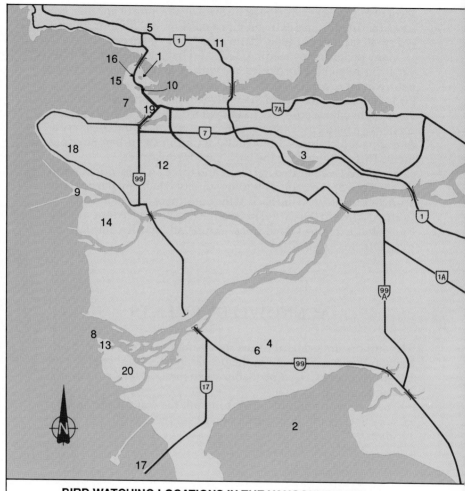

BIRD WATCHING LOCATIONS IN THE VANCOUVER AREA

1. Beaver Lake
2. Boundary Bay
3. Burnaby Lake
4. Burns Bog
5. Capilano River
6. Delta Garbage Dump
7. English Bay

8. George C. Reifel
   Migratory Bird Sanctuary
9. Iona Island
10. Lost Lagoon
11. North Shore Mountains
12. Queen Elizabeth Park
13. Reifel Island

14. Sea Island
15. Siwash Rock
16. Stanley Park
17. Tsawwassen Ferry Terminal
18. University of British Columbia
    Endowment Lands
19. Vancouver City Centre
20. Westham Island

BIRDS IN THE CITY

Birds provide a very real and tangible way of identifying with nature. Whether on a busy downtown city street or in a remote wildlife sanctuary, there are birds around us that are comparatively easy to see and to appreciate — without the need for special knowledge or equipment. Over the last decade more and more people have taken up birdwatching in their spare time, and today it is the fastest growing recreational activity in the western world. Whether actually going out on a hike to look for birds, or merely enjoying them as part of another recreational activity, birdwatching greatly enhances our appreciation for the environment and our enjoyment of the outdoors.

Most of us in British Columbia live in cities or towns, but this in no way diminishes the opportunities for pleasure in looking for birds. Many birds have adapted to the urban situation, and their variety and abundance in the city can be surprising. A few urban areas resemble natural habitats, and the limiting factors that most affect birds are the pressure of human disturbance and the availability of suitable feeding and nesting areas. Some of the more hardy and adaptable birds, such as House Sparrows, starlings, and Rock Doves (pigeons), have adapted so well to living along-side humans that they are sometimes considered pests. Neverthe-less, these common birds provide a welcome presence on the urban scene.

The back yard is one of the best places to watch birds; it provides people with a real opportunity to bring birds into their lives and to attract them out into the open. But it is by no means the only place in the Vancouver area to see birds. Some of the urban parks and wildlife sanctuaries are truly natural areas and in these settings it is possible to see a vast variety of species that do not readily spring to mind as city birds — warblers, flycatchers, hawks, ducks and owls.

Even downtown city parks like Stanley Park can provide some intriguing and enjoyable opportunities for observing the ways of birds which have adapted to city life. Birds such as Rock Doves and House Sparrows have adapted so well to inner city life that they have extended their breeding seasons well into the colder months, by taking advantage of situations provided by humans. A warm sheltered ledge on an office building provides pigeons with a centrally heated nesting site, and it is not uncommon for these birds to breed throughout the year. Other birds make use of man-made nesting locations: starlings and swallows will use a variety of odd sites, nesting under the eaves of a house, or even choosing a hole in a street lamp. Peregrine Falcons may nest on tall buildings and Barn Owls may nest under bridges in the middle of the city.

To fully appreciate the variety and abundance of bird life in the city, venture out into the natural areas that have been conserved in our urban environment. The birds that are to be found around Vancouver are those which are looking for habitats similar to the natural areas outside the city, so select the habitat for the type of birds you hope to watch and the chances of a rewarding bird-watching sortie will be much improved.

Vancouver is a coastal city with many different natural habitats at its doorstep — coastal rainforest, rocky shore, sandy shore, estuary, freshwater marsh and river — all within a few miles of the city centre. There are also many urban equivalents of these habi-tats: a well wooded neighbourhood will attract many of the forest birds, and a rocky breakwater is likely to attract birds of the shore.

The best tactic is to decide on a series of habitats to visit on an outing, and go to areas where you know these habitats exist. Not surprisingly, the areas where there are mixtures of habitats will increase the likelihood of seeing more species of birds. Wet areas with open water, surrounded by native trees, will provide some of the richest of urban birdwatching experiences.

HABITATS

Within the city, there are many semi-natural and natural areas that are remnants of the untouched, unspoiled landscape that existed before this part of British Columbia became increasingly settled, mostly during the last 150 years. The managed parks within the city are by no means natural to this part of Canada, but they provide birds and humans alike with a green oasis in the city which can be used in the absence of any really natural areas. However, the best spots for the birdwatcher to explore are those that most closely resemble the more natural areas of the province.

Coastal Forest

Before the Europeans came to this area, coastal rainforest dominated the vegetation. For thousands of years, tree growth had been unimpeded, except by storms and age. It is hard to imagine the spectacular sight that must have met the early visitors to the area: a vista of untouched coastal forest surrounding the expanse of the Fraser River, where now stands a vast city. Although most of the natural forest has gone, we do have small areas within the city, or close by, that have been carefully protected. These give us a good idea of what the forest was like. The wonderful woodlands in the University Endowment Lands, Stanley Park, Lynn Canyon and Lighthouse Park, are all remnants of a main forest that was once more widespread.

The most common trees are the massive Douglas firs, western red cedars and western hemlocks. Beneath them are smaller species such as red alder and broadleaf maple. Much of the coastal forest has a rich understorey of shrubs and other flowering plants, as well as many different kinds of fern. It is no wonder that this rich and varied vegetation supports a unique bird fauna. Bald Eagles and other birds of prey nest in the tall trees, woodpeckers use the abundant woodlands for nesting cavities and the dense shrub and ground cover is wonderful habitat for wrens, thrushes and other smaller birds. The treetops support noisy flocks of kinglets, chickadees, nuthatches and warblers. This exciting forest is available for the enjoyment of all of us living in and around Vancouver.

The Coast

There are a number of different coastal habitats which are quite distinct. Broadly speaking, these are sandy shore, rocky shore, river estuary and open saltwater. Within the city is the protected deep water of the harbour, which is an excellent birdwatching area. Open, exposed marine waters can be experienced best by taking a ferry trip to Vancouver Island.

Boundary Bay, south of Vancouver, has the most sandy shore habitat. It is here that many species of shorebirds will be found in the spring and autumn, as they stop over on migration to and from their breeding grounds. Next time you go to the beach, consider going earlier in the day, before most people get there, and you may well be rewarded with some good birdwatching. It is worthwhile to time your visits just ahead of an incoming tide, and let the tides bring the birds to you. In the middle of the day, it is worth looking for cormorants, gulls and sea ducks off shore.

The natural rocky shores and man-made breakwaters and sea walls, such as around Stanley Park and off Tsawwassen, are very different habitats than sandy areas. This is an important environment for some birds. Black Turnstones and Rock Sandpipers spend most of their time here, feeding on small marine animals such as snails, limpets and mussels which hide in rock crevices, adhere strongly to the rocks, or hide amongst the seaweed. Birds have evolved specialized feeding strategies and adaptations, such as strong beaks, to be able to exploit these animals.

To be able to nest on this sort of shore also requires a degree of specialization. On rocky shores with vertical cliffs, such as Siwash Rock in Stanley Park, seabirds may be found breeding. The Pelagic Cormorant builds its seaweed nest on a precarious ledge, the Glaucous-winged Gull builds its grass nest on a gentle slope, and the black and white Pigeon Guillemot simply lays its eggs, without building a nest, deep in a rock crevice.

Rocky shore usually gives us a vantage point from which to see out over the water, and the water at this point is usually deep: take advantage of this to watch for loons, grebes, diving ducks and diving seabirds such as murrelets, not normally seen this close to shore.

The estuary is yet another coastal habitat. The Fraser River flows into the sea near Vancouver and provides us with one of the most important habitats for birds on the west coast of North America. The Fraser River estuary is a refuelling point for hundreds of thousands of migrating shorebirds and waterfowl. Perhaps the best place to learn about the estuary is at the George C. Reifel Migratory Bird Sanctuary west of Ladner. There is a small visitor centre there, and an observation tower which looks out over the marsh. The sanctuary is also a good place to meet other birdwatchers.

Freshwater Marshes

Any habitat where there is open freshwater or even a damp marshy area is attractive to all sorts of birds. Some birds, such as the ducks, geese, coots, rails, blackbirds and wrens, feed and breed in these habitats while others, such as gulls, come to drink and bathe. Lost Lagoon in Stanley Park in the centre of the city, or Burnaby and Deer Lakes east of Vancouver, are the best places to visit. There are many less obvious kinds of wetland habitats which are important to birds as well, such as the small artificial ponds in city parks, drainage ditches, temporary puddles in fields and even fish ponds. In these, look for Great Blue Herons, Red-winged Blackbirds, Belted Kingfishers and ducks.

Rivers

Another wetland habitat near Vancouver is the clear, fast flowing, rocky rivers, such as the Lynn and Capilano Rivers on the north shore mountains. These waterways are sheltered and damp and attract many forest species as well as some specialized waterbirds, such as the American Dipper and Common Merganser. Even Harlequin Ducks have been found breeding here in summer.

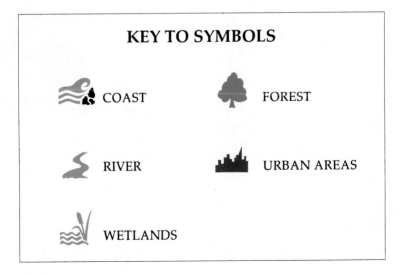

KEY TO SYMBOLS

COAST

FOREST

RIVER

URBAN AREAS

WETLANDS

BEACHES AND BAYS

Sandy beaches and protected marine waters in bays, within easy walking distance of the centre of the city, attract a wide variety of waterbirds, waders, scavengers and predators.

LOST LAGOON IN STANLEY PARK
This brackish lagoon, set in a park-like environment and surrounded by tall coniferous trees, is an oasis for migrating and breeding waterbirds. At noon each day many Vancouver business people visit the area to watch and feed the birds.

GEORGE C. REIFEL
MIGRATORY BIRD SANCTUARY

Extensive saltwater marshes, quiet ponds and sloughs, agricultural fields and wooded hedgerows are homes for over 300 species of birds at this popular wildlife refuge.

ROCKY SHORES
Rocky cliffs and offshore islands in Stanley Park, and just north of the city proper, support nesting seabirds from May through August. In winter, many colourful diving ducks feed here on marine snails, clams, mussels and fishes.

CAPILANO RIVER

The rain forest of Stanley Park and the north shore mountains is home to a group of secretive birds, challenging to spot, but easy to hear. Look along the crystal clear creeks and rivers for dippers, thrushes and occasionally Harlequin Ducks. *(right)*

QUEEN ELIZABETH PARK

Open spaces, with native and exotic trees and shrubs, provide homes and feeding areas for a variety of songbirds. The Observatory is a good spot to watch migration in progress in both spring and fall. *(below)*

COMMON LOON

Gavia immer

larger than seagull-sized

THE BIRD ON OUR DOLLAR COIN is the common loon, a bird that epitomizes Canada's wilderness. It has two distinct plumages. In summer the large black bill, black velvety head with a white necklace, and black back with small checkered white spots, are distinctive. In winter, the bird is generally a uniform brown-black above and white below.

The Common Loon is present around Vancouver throughout the year, but it is mostly common from mid-October to mid-May. Sometimes loose flocks, up to twenty or so birds, may be seen in spring (late April) and autumn (mid-September to mid-October) migration periods, but most sightings are of single birds. It frequents sea coasts, bays, and the lower reaches of the Fraser River. The waters off the Stanley Park seawall are a very good spot to find this large bird.

Loons dive for fish, often swimming to depths of fifty-five to sixty metres, propelled by their powerful webbed feet. Most dives last less than thirty seconds, but can last up to three minutes. Common Loons feed mainly on sculpins, Pacific Herring, and other small near-shore fishes.

PIED-BILLED GREBE

Podilymbus podiceps
smaller than crow-sized

THE PIED-BILLED GREBE is a small, dumpy, brown water bird, with a short neck and a short, stout bill. During the breeding season, it has a black throat patch and a black ring around a whitish bill, from which it gets its name.

Pied-billed grebes are present throughout the year but are much more numerous from September to April when migrating birds from the interior of British Columbia make their way to the coast to pass the winter. They are found on saltwater but, unlike our other wintering grebes, are mostly found near brackish and freshwater lakes, sloughs and marshes. Burnaby Lake and the George C. Reifel Migratory Bird Sanctuary are the best places to search. The Ladner area south of Vancouver has the highest number of Pied-billed Grebes reported in British Columbia during Christmas bird counts.

This grebe can often be shy, keeping close to the vegetation around the edges of the water; this is where to look for them. The birds are often seen with American Coots, and some puddle ducks. They feed on a wide variety of prey but mostly small fishes, aquatic insects and snails.

HORNED GREBE

Podiceps auritus
smaller than crow-sized

THE COLOURS OF THIS SMALL GREBE are entirely different between seasons, except for the red eye. In summer it is a striking bird with a rufous neck, black head with yellow ear tufts and dark back with rusty brown sides. In winter it is drab, generally dark grey-brown above and white below, including the cheek, throat and breast.

It is chiefly a saltwater bird of near-shore areas where it can be found regularly from late September through March. Look for the Horned Grebe off Stanley Park, in English Bay, near the Tsawwassan ferry terminal, or in the Fraser River near the Deas Tunnel. Don't look for flocks; this species is solitary in its habits.

In winter the Horned Grebe feeds entirely on fishes and marine invertebrates such as snails, small clams and crustaceans. It dives in waters to nine metres depth and averages about 25 seconds underwater. Occasionally groups of five or more will feed as a team, diving together to surround a school of small fishes.

WESTERN GREBE
Aechmophorus occidentalis
seagull-sized

VANCOUVER OWNS A WORLD RECORD! More Western Grebes spend the winter here than anywhere else in the world. Each year up to 15,000 birds can be seen in English Bay off Kitsilano Beach, strung out in a long line or feeding together in a large, dense flock. Small flocks can also be found off Stanley Park, in Deas Slough, and in the lower reaches of the Fraser River.

This waterbird is easy to identify. It has a long, slender, black-and-white neck, swan-like in appearance. Generally it is dark above and white below and, like other grebes, sits low in the water. The thin bill is long and pointed.

This grebe dives for fish, sometimes staying underwater for a minute or so. It pierces prey with its sharp bill. It feeds mainly in the early morning.

Birds which winter off Vancouver arrive each autumn from nesting colonies in central British Columbia, as well as Alberta and Saskatchewan.

DOUBLE-CRESTED CORMORANT

Phalacrocorax auritus
larger than seagull-sized

BRANDT'S CORMORANT

Phalacrocorax penicillatus
larger than seagull-sized

PELAGIC CORMORANT

Phalacrocorax pelagicus
seagull-sized

OFTEN CALLED "EITHER-ENDERS," cormorants are amongst the most common and easily identified of all seabird groups around the Vancouver waterfront. The three species can be told apart in flight with a little practice. The Pelagic Cormorant, the smallest and most common of the three, is slender in flight and has a very straight neck, a small head, and a rapid wing beat. Brandt's, the rarest, is stockier, with a large head and a straight neck, while the Double-crested Cormorant is stocky, with a thick neck and large head. It flies with a heavy wing beat and often with a distinct kink in the neck. Up close, look for the differently coloured throat patches: yellow to orange in Double-crested, red in Pelagic, and blue in Brandt's, but with buff-coloured throat feathers. In late spring and summer Brandt's also shows long white feathers on the neck and back, the Double-crested develops two white ear tufts, while the Pelagic Cormorant sports two white flank patches.

Of the two species which breed near Vancouver, the Double-crested Cormorant is less numerous. Several pairs have recently started to nest on the rocky breakwater and atop wooden pilings near the Tsawwassen ferry terminal, and their large, bulky stick nests can be seen with binoculars. The Pelagic Cormorant prefers narrow ledges on steep cliffs in Stanley Park. (Don't look skyward when strolling beneath the nests along the seawall!) Several pairs also build their seaweed nests on Siwash Rock here.

Although all three species are present throughout the year around Vancouver, winter is the best time to see them. The Double-crested Cormorant is best seen on wooden pilings and log booms in the mouth of the Fraser River. The Brandt's Cormorant can be seen near the Tsawwassen ferry terminal, although the best vantage point is from the ferry itself which passes through a major wintering spot in Active Pass, about mid-point in the trip between

Top: *Double-crested Cormorant*
Left: *Pelagic Cormorant*
Bottom: *Brandt's Cormorant*

the mainland and Vancouver Island. The marine environment around Stanley Park is the best location to view the Pelagic Cormorant.

Unlike other waterbirds, the webbed feet of cormorants are unusual in that the web connects four toes instead of three. This allows the birds to cling to rocky cliffs as well as pursue shoaling fish such as Pacific herring and sandlance, or locate solitary fish hiding among seaweeds or under rocks.

GREAT BLUE HERON
Ardea herodias

larger than seagull-sized

HERE IN VANCOUVER, Great Blue Herons are present throughout the year. They are distinctive in flight, as they trail their long legs behind them and carry their necks bent in an S-shape. The birds are large, about 1.2 m tall, with a wingspan of 2.1 m, and generally have a blue-grey body. Frequently the Great Blue Heron is mistaken for a Sandhill Crane, which is very rare in Vancouver.

Herons can be found wherever there is shallow water or in open short-grass fields. In winter, large numbers can be seen in knee-deep water over mud flats, especially off the Tsawwassen ferry terminal. In summer, birdwatchers are attracted to their nesting colony in Stanley Park. This heronry, in the zoo, is the oldest in British Columbia.

The Great Blue Heron is a patient hunter, whether standing in water waiting for a fish to appear, or in a dry field waiting for a mouse to come within striking distance. It catches its prey, which also includes frogs, snakes, crabs and insects, with a lightning thrust of the beak. At times, when the prey seems longer than the heron is capable of eating, swallowing can take several minutes.

MUTE SWAN

Cygnus olor

larger than seagull-sized

THE MUTE SWAN, originally from Europe and Asia, was first introduced into British Columbia, at Victoria, about 1889. In Vancouver it is only found as a captive bird in the Lost Lagoon in Stanley Park. On adjacent Vancouver Island, feral populations exist.

This large white swan often arches its wings over its back, particularly when displaying or behaving aggressively. The pinkish or orange bill with a black knob at its base is characteristic. Two other species of swans likely to be seen in rural farmlands south of the city, as they migrate to and from their breeding grounds, are the Tundra Swan and the Trumpeter Swan. The former usually has a small yellow spot on the black bill, the latter a solid black bill. In addition, the Mute Swan is less vocal than the others, usually making only a hissing sound. It is the only one likely to be seen within Vancouver itself.

The Mute Swan builds a very large nest of grasses, reeds, and cattails, usually in shallow water. Up to eight eggs may be laid in early April but most egg-laying occurs in late May and early June. It takes up to 150 days before the young can fly. It is not wise to venture near a nesting swan as there are many instances of people being attacked and hurt.

SNOW GOOSE
Anser caerulescens
larger than seagull-sized

THE WILDLIFE SPECTACLE of the year occurs each autumn when thousands of Snow Geese return to the marshes of the Fraser River delta to spend the winter. Birds from Alaska and Russia begin arriving in October and reach peak numbers in November when up to 40,000 geese may be present. Their noise is deafening. The best place to view them is from the observation tower or the outer marsh trails of the George C. Reifel Migratory Bird Sanctuary.

The adult Snow Goose is all white except for its wing tips which show black just above the tail when it is at rest. The legs are pink, as is the bill. Immatures are generally dusky gray on the back and whitish below. The Snow Goose has a black stripe on the side of its beak, which gives it a comical grinning appearance.

Banding studies have shown that most of the migrant and winter visitors to the delta marshes south of Vancouver are from breeding colonies on Wrangel Island in the U.S.S.R.

CANADA GOOSE

Branta canadensis

larger than seagull-sized

THERE ARE MANY DIFFERENT SUBSPECIES of this bird which, with practice, can be separated by size, colour and voice. Four of these have been seen in the Vancouver area, mostly in the spring and autumn when they are on migration. Most common is the western race, which is a darker brown and lacks the noticeably pale breast of the others.

Canada Geese can be found here at any time of the year, as many have become semi-tame and will vie with Mallards, Glaucous-winged Gulls and American Coots for scraps of bread and bird seed. It is also possible to see truly wild geese, especially during migration. Farmlands south of Vancouver city are good places to watch for them. Lost Lagoon in Stanley Park is a popular area to feed geese.

The Canada Goose builds its grass nest on the ground, usually near water. The female lines the nest with down from her breast and uses the down to cover the eggs, keeping them warm and drawing less attention to them when the adults leave the nest. Up to fourteen eggs may be laid, usually in late April, but sometimes as early as mid-March. Incubation takes 28 days, and another 63 days are required for full flight. Apparently many geese mate for life and sometimes family groups can be distinguished by careful observation during migration.

WOOD DUCK

Aix sponsa

crow-sized

THIS IS A PERCHING DUCK: it has sharp claws on its feet which grip tree branches and snags. The male is the most colourful duck in North America; its iridescent green head with white markings, and its crest and narrow red bill are unmistakable. The female, far less brightly coloured, is still one of the most attractively marked of the female ducks. Look for the white teardrop shape through the eye.

Wood Ducks can be seen throughout the year around Vancouver, although many of the breeding birds fly south to winter. Watch for them on any wooded lake or slough, and even in the city centre at Lost Lagoon and Beaver Lake in Stanley Park.

The Wood Duck is a hole-nesting duck, and it often uses deep cracks in trees and even the old nesting holes of the Pileated Woodpecker. It also takes readily to nesting boxes erected to attract it. Egg-laying occurs in April and May; first young could appear in mid-May. Within hours of hatching, the young use their sharp claws to climb up the inside of the nest hole and jump to the ground — unhurt. At one nest site in Stanley Park a pair of Wood Ducks used a natural cavity high up in a Douglas fir. On hatching, the ducklings fell sixteen metres and, with their mother, quickly waddled — unscathed — to nearby Beaver Lake.

MALLARD
Anas platyrhynchos
seagull-sized

THIS IS THE MOST ABUNDANT AND BEST KNOWN of all ducks, and readily adapts to people and city environments such as Vancouver's Stanley Park. The male Mallard is easily identified; look for the green head, "curly-tails" and iridescent blue feathers in the wing. The latter, called the "speculum," can be used to identify puddle-ducks, as it varies in colour from species to species. The female has the same orange legs as the male, but is otherwise brown, with a paler breast and underside.

Mallards are dabbling ducks, and when feeding, they often up-end to reach below the surface for waterweeds and other vegetation, seeds, grain, small insects and snails. Some Mallards are present year-round in Vancouver, but birds from the north and the interior also winter here — well over thirty thousand birds in the Greater Vancouver area.

The Mallard has a long breeding season on the south coast of British Columbia. Downy young can be found as early as March and as late as mid-November. Despite the fact that the female may already be paired, it is a common sight in the spring, especially in city parks, to see a hen pursued by three or more drakes.

NORTHERN PINTAIL
Anas acuta

seagull-sized

OF ALL DUCKS, the Northern Pintail is the most graceful and elegant. The male's plumage is striking, with its chestnut brown head, white neck and gray body, and long, thin black central tailfeathers. The female is a subtle mixture of browns. Both are easily recognized in flight from a distance by their long necks and pointed "pin" tails.

The species is most abundant during migration, especially in autumn when both young and adults pass through the Vancouver area in large flocks from August to late October. Each year tens of thousands stop and winter, especially in marshes and fields surrounding the Fraser River delta. The Northern Pintail breeds only in small numbers here.

The scientific name for this slender bird is derived from Latin words which mean "duck with a pointed tail." The Northern Pintail eats a variety of plants and animals but, while here, eats mostly farm crops and marsh vegetation.

NORTHERN SHOVELER
Anas clypeata
larger than crow-sized

THE MALE NORTHERN SHOVELER is a brightly coloured duck, a little smaller than a Mallard; it is a study in contrasts. A bright green head, chestnut flanks, a pure white breast and a black-and-white back make it an easy bird to recognize in a marsh. The female is a uniform mottled brown. The speculum on the wings of both sexes is green, unlike the iridescent blue wedge of the Mallard. The Northern Shoveler owes its name to its very large, spoon-shaped bill.

The Northern Shoveler is present throughout the year around Vancouver. It breeds here, from May to July, but is most common in the non-breeding season, from mid-October to the end of March. It can be found on any suitable shallow pond or lake, or with other waterfowl in flooded fields. Good viewing spots include Beaver Lake in Stanley Park, Burnaby Lake, Ladner Marshes, and of course the George C. Reifel Migratory Bird Sanctuary.

Shovelers are dabbling ducks, and feed in shallow water by sifting the surface water for both plant food, such as seeds of water plants, and for small aquatic animals. Its bill is wonderfully adapted for this; as well as being large, it has a sieve-like inside edge which enables the bird to screen its food from muddy water.

AMERICAN WIGEON
Anas americana
larger than crow-sized

THE MALE AMERICAN WIGEON is readily identified by the white on its forehead and crown, which gave the duck its old and not very flattering name of Baldpate. The female, as is often the case with ducks, is brown, an adaptation to avoid detection by predators during incubation. Both male and female have a striking white breast and large white wing patches, which are most visible when the birds are in flight.

The American Wigeon is an abundant winter resident on the south coast of British Columbia. Up to 65,000 birds are present from October through March in the marshes of the Fraser River delta. In some years this duck is the most numerous bird tallied on Christmas Bird Counts. A few pairs breed in the area each year.

Look for this puddle duck anywhere that large patches of grass are found, such as golf courses and parks. It also frequents sewage outlets, agricultural fields, and marshy habitats. This gregarious bird is predominantly vegetarian, grazing on grasses and sedges as well as on marine algae on the shoreline.

Each winter another rarer but closely related species, the Eurasian Wigeon *(A. penelope),* identified by its rusty-brown head, can be spotted among our flocks of American Wigeon.

GREATER SCAUP
Aythya marila
crow-sized

THERE ARE TWO SPECIES of scaup, or blue-bills, found in British Columbia, but the more common on saltwater is the Greater Scaup. Both species look almost identical and are always a problem to tell apart. Look for the more rounded head of the Greater Scaup (the Lesser Scaup's head appears more domed) and in good light, the male Greater Scaup's head shows a green gloss, compared to the blue or purple gloss of the Lesser Scaup. The females are brown and show a white patch at the base of the bill, a mark that is visible from quite a distance. In flight they present a very black and white look, and have a white trailing edge on the upper hind part of the wings. The white wing-stripe of the Greater Scaup extends through most of the wing.

The Greater Scaup is a common sight on the sea around Vancouver from November through March. It can be seen in most sheltered coastal areas, and off Stanley Park and Kitsilano Beach are good places to look. A few individuals of both species remain in Vancouver waters through the summer, but don't breed.

HARLEQUIN DUCK
Histrionicus histrionicus
crow-sized

STANLEY PARK'S SHORELINE is a good place to see this brightly patterned duck. Only the male Wood Duck rivals it as the "best dressed waterfowl." The grey-blue body of the male is boldly marked with white stripes and spots on the breast, back of the head, base of the bill and behind the eye. These contrast beautifully with the rich chestnut flanks. The female is generally a subdued grey-brown, with a dusky light belly and with two or three spots on the head.

The Harlequin Duck is fairly common throughout the year anywhere rocky shorelines are found, especially in the vicinity of Stanley Park and north shore river-mouths, such as the Capilano River. In April pairs fly to freshwater streams on the north shore mountains to breed. In May, males return to Stanley Park to moult out of their garish nuptial plumage, leaving the females on the fast-flowing streams to incubate the eggs and raise the brood.

Harlequins feed on a variety of marine invertebrates that are common on rocky shallows. Small snails, worms, mussels, clams, crabs and other crustaceans make up their diet.

SURF SCOTER
Melanitta perspicillata
larger than crow-sized

THE SURF SCOTER is an attractive, large sea duck. The male is black, except for a white patch on the back of the neck and the top of the head. It has orangish feet and legs, and its bill is large and brightly marked with black, white and orange. The female is much drabber and is largely brown, with some white behind the bill and below the eye.

Surf Scoters are found on saltwater. Although they are essentially a winter duck in Coastal British Columbia, many non-breeding birds remain in the Greater Vancouver area year round. Spring departures, for northern breeding grounds, occur mainly in April. By September, many will have returned to the coastal waters around Vancouver, especially off Stanley Park and in Boundary Bay.

Watch for Surf Scoters in shallow marine and brackish areas, and in the rough water well offshore — as their name implies. Groups of thousands may be watched feeding on mussels and clams, which they wrestle from rocks or prod from sandy sea floors.

WHITE-WINGED SCOTER
Melanitta fusca
larger than crow-sized

LARGEST OF THE DUCKS found in British Columbia, the White-winged Scoter is a sea duck and, except during the breeding season, is found almost exclusively on saltwater. The male is essentially black, with a small white mark through the eye and a white patch on each wing. This white can be hidden at times but is very noticeable in flight, and is a good way of distinguishing the species. The female is a fairly uniform dark brown and shows the white wing patch as well.

The White-winged Scoter frequents marine and brackish waters throughout the year and is often found with rafts of Surf Scoters. The peak movement to breeding grounds in spring occurs in April; the return in autumn peaks in September. This bird is often seen in the calmer waters off Stanley Park, in the Fraser River and in Boundary Bay.

During the winter, it feeds by diving for clams, snails, barnacles and crabs which are abundant along the coast. It uses its wings to reach prey, and prefers more shallow feeding sites than does the Surf Scoter.

COMMON GOLDENEYE
Bucephala clangula
crow-sized

BARROW'S GOLDENEYE
Bucephala islandica
crow-sized

BOTH SPECIES OF GOLDENEYES are seen around Vancouver throughout the year, but are most common during the winter months. Identifying males is easy. The Barrow's Goldeneye (next page) has a comma-shaped white patch on the face, compared to the round white patch in the Common Goldeneye (above); the back of the Barrow's is black, spotted with white, and in the Common Goldeneye the back appears much whiter. The Barrow's Goldeneye has a dark line of feathers that separates the white breast from the white flanks, whereas the white in the Common Goldeneye is continuous. The females, however, are difficult to tell apart; look for the Barrow's Goldeneye's steeper forehead and shorter, more orange bill.

Both species frequent a variety of marine and fresh water habitats. The Common Goldeneye is widely distributed along all

41

types of shoreline whereas the Barrow's Goldeneye frequents mainly rocky shorelines. Both species, however, can be seen together off Stanley Park. Southern coastal areas support the highest number of wintering Barrow's Goldeneyes in the world, and it is estimated that British Columbia has sixty to ninety percent of the world's breeding population.

Barrow's Goldeneye

BUFFLEHEAD
Bucephala albeola
smaller than crow-sized

THIS IS A SMALL DIVING DUCK that is related to the goldeneyes. Buffleheads do not breed here around Vancouver. However, large numbers arrive in the fall to spend the winter on estuaries, rivers, lakes and sloughs, and even on the sea. During the winter, they can be seen on virtually any body of water around Vancouver — even outdoor swimming pools!

The males are a sharply contrasting pattern of black and white, with iridescent purples and greens refracting from the black portion of the head. The females are dark brown and have white patches on the head. White on the inner edges of the wings is prominent in flight.

The Bufflehead dives for small snails, insects and animal larvae in freshwater habitats, but prefers clams, snails, amphipods and worms in saltwater feeding areas. It is estimated that about one-quarter of all Buffleheads wintering in British Columbia can be found in the Greater Vancouver area.

COMMON MERGANSER

Mergus merganser

larger than seagull-sized

SURPRISINGLY, THIS SAW-BILLED DUCK is commonly mistaken for a Mallard. Although males of both species have green heads, the merganser is larger, longer and more slender in profile with a characteristic long thin red bill and pure white breast and sides. The female has a brown head with conspicuous crest, white breast, and greyish back. Also, mergansers are entirely fish eaters. Their beaks are finely "toothed," which enables them to catch and hold prey which is swallowed whole.

The Common Merganser is present in the Vancouver area throughout the year, but is most numerous from November through March. At this time, flocks of up to one hundred birds can be found in river channels, on larger lakes, and during very cold winters on the sea when lakes are frozen. A few pair nest along mountain streams each summer.

Its relative, the Red-breasted Merganser, has a head crest, reddish-brown breast, and grey sides in the male, while females of the two species are very difficult to differentiate. Here, the sharp division between the head and breast in the Common Merganser is the most reliable identification feature.

Inset: female

BALD EAGLE
Haliaeetus leucocephalus
larger than seagull-szied

THIS LARGE BIRD OF PREY can be seen throughout the year, even near the centre of the city. The adult is distinctive with its pure white head and tail. The young bird, however, is much more difficult to identify and may be confused with the rarer Golden Eagle. Both have dark brown bodies, but the Bald Eagle lacks the broad white band at the base of the tail, found in immature Golden Eagles. It is five years before Bald Eagles obtain full adult plumage.

Bald Eagles are most common near water and will often spend hours sitting on a snag overlooking the sea or river marshes. They are adept at catching not only fish, but large birds like Great Blue Herons, Snow and Canada Geese, Ring-necked Pheasants, and Glaucous-winged Gulls. They also feed on carrion found along the shore.

Bald Eagles build huge stick nests in trees and will often re-use a nest year after year, the nest eventually reaching an immense size. The largest nest measured 3.6 m in diameter and 3 m in height. Eggs may be laid from mid-February through late June and it is rare to find young still in the nest after mid-August. The nearest nest to Vancouver centre is located near Lost Lagoon in Stanley Park.

NORTHERN HARRIER
Circus cyaneus

larger than crow-sized

FORMERLY KNOWN AS MARSH HAWK, this abundant bird of prey is always found in open habitats such as marshes, grass fields, and log-littered beaches. You won't find it in the centre of the city but you will be able to see it on the outskirts of Vancouver. It is present throughout the year but highest numbers are found from December through April. In fact, more harriers winter in the Fraser River delta than anywhere else in Canada.

Unlike many birds of prey, sexes are differently coloured. Each has long narrow wings and tail and shows a white rump patch in flight. Males (below), however, are grey overall while females are generally rust-brown in colour. They feed on small mammals, birds and snakes.

Northern Harriers nest anywhere that large tracts of cattails, tall grasses or low bushes are found. Eggs are laid in a ground nest in late April and early May and hatch in June.

SHARP-SHINNED HAWK

Accipiter striatus

larger than robin-sized

THIS TINY HAWK is typically seen in woodland areas around the edges of the city. It is about the same size as, or a little larger than, a jay. As in most hawks, there is quite a difference in size, the female being larger. Adults have dark blue-grey upperparts while the underparts are light and barred with red-brown. The similar Cooper's Hawk is larger and shows a rounded tip to the tail instead of the more squarish shape of the Sharp-shinned Hawk.

The Sharp-shinned Hawk normally builds its nest of twigs in a coniferous tree. The birds are secretive and inconspicuous most of the time, but during the breeding season they are more vociferous near their nests. They hunt small birds by chasing them at high speeds through much denser cover than most birds of prey, and their long tails serve as a rudder to help them manoeuvre at high speed. During autumn migration, Sharp-shinned Hawks can be seen along mountains to the north of the city, where they take advantage of thermals to help them fly south. They are also quick to appreciate a well-visited feeder, so position feeders where smaller birds have an escape route into a nearby bush or tree.

AMERICAN KESTREL
Falco sparverius
smaller than robin-sized

THIS SMALL FALCON used to be known as the Sparrow Hawk. It is the only North American falcon that has different plumages between males and females. Both sexes are very attractive birds with distinctive double moustache marks. The male has an orange-brown back and tail; its wings are a slate blue. The female has a much deeper red-brown tone to its upperparts, including the wings.

American Kestrels are migratory in British Columbia, although a few overwinter in the outskirts of Vancouver. The males are the first to arrive in spring, in late April. The males seek out and defend a breeding territory and within a couple of weeks, the females arrive. The pair nest in tree cavities — often abandoned woodpecker holes, natural tree cavities -- and frequently they will use a nesting box. Eggs are laid in late April and hatch about a month later. Once the young birds fledge, they stay with their parents in a family group and can often be seen on telephone wires, fence posts and light standards around the city outskirts. Large insects and mice are the usual prey. The American Kestrel characteristically hunts by hovering and then swooping down onto its prey.

MERLIN
Falco columbarius
larger than robin-sized

FORMERLY KNOWN AS THE PIGEON HAWK, the Merlin is a small dark falcon with long pointed wings. It does not have the typical moustache marks of other falcons, nor the bold plumage patterns. The birds around Vancouver belong to a race that breeds along the west coast of British Columbia and are darker than those found in the rest of Canada.

The Merlin is the most adaptable of the four species of falcons found around Vancouver. It is as much at home in the middle of the city chasing birds at feeders as it is hunting shorebirds along beaches. It can often be seen in the late afternoon chasing starlings as they come onto bridges to roost for the evening.

A few birds remain each summer to nest but most are migratory, passing through in spring in early April and in autumn in late September and early October. From November through February is the best time to spot this bird. Keep your eyes open as you may only catch a fleeting glimpse of a Merlin passing at high speed.

PEREGRINE FALCON
Falco peregrinus
crow-sized

BIRDWATCHERS IN VANCOUVER have a good chance of seeing a peregrine falcon, especially from September through February. In flight, look for a bird with narrow, pointed wings and a shallow but rapid wing beat. When perched, notice the moustache stripe and the slate-grey backs of the adults and brown backs of the immature falcons. Underparts are barred in adults and streaked in immatures.

The Peregrine Falcon feeds on medium-sized birds, including small shorebirds and pigeons, and larger perching birds like starlings. It catches prey by direct pursuit from a power dive. This method involves the Peregrine's circling under a flock of birds to force them to a great height, whereupon he will casually break away. As the flock returns downward, the Peregrine will "stoop" with great speed, singling out a victim before it can reach the safety of the trees. Look for Peregrines wherever large numbers of prey gather — along the seashore or over fields.

Between 100 and 110 pairs of Peregrine Falcons breed in British Columbia, mostly on the Queen Charlotte Islands. However, a few pairs breed in the Gulf Islands. Fortunately, in British Columbia there is no evidence to suggest that DDT has affected the reproductive success of this once-threatened species.

RING-NECKED PHEASANT
Phasianus colchicus
larger than seagull-sized

ORIGINALLY AN ASIAN BIRD, the Ring-necked Pheasant was introduced to farmlands south of Vancouver in 1880 as a sporting bird. Additional introductions occurred until 1950. Since then, the population has increased, partly through the expansion of wild populations and partly through provincial government breeding programs. Today, the spectacular plumage of the male is a familiar sight in the fields around the edge of the city. It may even be seen in tidal marshes, secluded wooded parks and brushy areas around golf courses.

During the spring breeding season, the males collect a harem of up to five hens, which they then attempt to protect from the advances of male rivals. The females are much less gaudily coloured than their mates. They incubate the eggs, which have been laid in a grass-lined depression on the ground — often hidden below a bush. The size of a normal clutch varies, but usually consists of 9 to 13 olive-brown eggs. Sometimes more than one female will lay in the same nest and eggs will literally overflow the edges. Twenty-eight eggs are the most that have been found in one nest in British Columbia. When this happens, very few actually hatch.

AMERICAN COOT
Fulica americana
smaller than crow-sized

THIS CHICKEN-LIKE BIRD, most frequently found on marshy lakes and sloughs around the city, is readily identified by its behaviour and markings. It bobs its head as it walks and swims, making it look like a comical clockwork toy. Its generally blackish plumage is highlighted by a white bill and white patch under its short tail. Its toes are lobed and flattened to help with swimming and walking on mud, from which it derives its popular western name, "mudhen."

It is most common here in winter. Autumn migrants begin arriving in late September and numbers increase throughout October and into November, especially at Burnaby Lake and the George C. Reifel Migratory Bird Sanctuary. A few can also be seen on Lost Lagoon in Stanley Park. By early April, only a few breeding pairs remain.

American Coots feed by diving and tipping for water weeds, small shellfish and shrimps. They also search the edges of ponds and sloughs for insects and snails. They build a floating nest of reeds and rushes amongst the vegetation at the edge of the water and by late May, lay 8 to 12 spotted, buff-coloured eggs. Young hatch in about twenty-three days.

BLACK-BELLIED PLOVER

Pluvialis squatarola

larger than robin-sized

YOU WILL HAVE TO TRAVEL outside the city proper to see the Black-bellied Plover — to the mud flats and fields of the Fraser River delta. The best times to find this shorebird are from late April through early May, and in September and October. Up to 1,000 birds are present during the winter, but they are more difficult to locate then.

In the spring, look for a generally grey bird, in flocks, with a black throat and belly, and a white top to its head and white under its tail. The back is mottled black and white. In autumn, it is a very different bird: a uniform mottled grey on its back, with a paler grey underside. In all plumages, it has a short black bill and long black legs and when it flies, its white rump and black "armpits" are distinctive. Plan your visit at high tide when the plovers are pushed closer to shore.

Like many shorebirds the Black-bellied Plover feeds in a typical stop-run-pick manner. On its Arctic breeding ground it feeds mainly on insects but in migration it turns to worms, small clams and crustaceans.

KILLDEER
Charadrius vociferus
robin-sized

THE KILLDEER is the most widespread of all shorebirds within the immediate area of the city. A relatively large plover, it is readily identified by its double black breast bands and by its call, *kildee kildee*, after which it is named. Its Latin name, *vociferus*, is no misnomer; it can be heard throughout the year and spends a great deal of time calling.

The Killdeer does not build a nest as such, but digs out a small scrape in the ground which it decorates with small stones, wood chips and pieces of plants. Typically it lays four buff-coloured eggs, well camouflaged with black spots, and may nest twice each summer. The Killdeer has refined the art of decoying predators away from the nest. It will trail a wing and drag a leg under the nose of a would-be predator, only to fly or run off at high speed once it has led the predator away from the nest site. It will even settle onto an imaginary nest, to try and lure the predator away. The Killdeer breeds on old industrial sites and gravel rooftops, as well as on unpaved roads, near golf courses and in any relatively open areas, including city gardens. It is resident in Vancouver, but numbers are greatest during spring and fall migration.

BLACK OYSTERCATCHER

Haematopus bachmani
larger than crow-sized

THE BLACK OYSTERCATCHER cannot be confused with any other
bird. It is a crow-sized, dull black wading bird, with a long,
relatively heavy red bill. Long pink legs and feet, and a red eye-
ring visible at close range, are also distinctive features.

This is a bird of the western rocky shores from Alaska to
Southern California. It is resident on the British Columbia coast-
line but is rare in Vancouver. Look for it in Stanley Park from
August to March. It breeds above the tide line on offshore islands
and breakwaters, and hardly bothers to build a nest at all, but
rather decorates a shallow depression — even on bare rock — with
pieces of shell and stones. Two or three well camouflaged, spotted
eggs are laid. The adults are vociferous at the best of times, but if
you happen to wander near a nest they become very noisy indeed.

The Black Oystercatcher feeds mainly on limpets and chitons
which it knocks off rocks at tide's edge. It also probes mussel beds
for other marine invertebrates and uses its laterally compressed
bill (slimmer side to side than top to bottom) to open bivalves such
as mussels, clams and oysters.

GREATER YELLOWLEGS
Tringa melanoleuca
smaller than crow-sized

THIS LARGE SANDPIPER sports its characteristic long, yellow legs in both breeding and winter plumage. It can be confused only with its smaller relative, the Lesser Yellowlegs *(T. flavipes)*, whose bill is thin and about equal to the head in length. The longer bill of the Greater Yellowlegs has a slight upward curve. Both species show white rumps when flying and both lack wing stripes. The Greater Yellowlegs usually occurs singly or in small flocks while the Lesser Yellowlegs is far more gregarious — flocks can number in the hundreds.

In Vancouver the Greater Yellowlegs has been found in every month of the year but is most numerous during spring migration (mid-April to early May) and during autumn migration (early July to late August). While migrating, both Yellowleg species may be seen feeding and resting together in the shallows of lakes, ponds, wet fields and tidal mud flats. Like many shorebirds, they can be approached quite closely, providing a good opportunity for one to appreciate the subtle details of form and behaviour.

SPOTTED SANDPIPER

Actitis macularia

smaller than robin-sized

THE SPOTTED SANDPIPER is perhaps the most widely distributed of all the wading birds in Canada. It is a small bird and, as its name suggests, has a spotted breast — but only during the summer breeding period. In winter, it loses the spotting and the breast becomes dull white. It is most often seen along the shores of ponds, lakes and rivers, and on grassy beaches.

The easiest way of identifying the Spotted Sandpiper is by its behaviour. It has a peculiar way of bobbing its whole body as it runs along. When disturbed, it usually gives a short call — *weet weet weet* — and flies out over the water to land a little further along the shore. Its flight is distinctive: it holds its wings slightly downward and flies with very stiff, rapid wing beats.

Like most shorebirds, this is a ground-nesting bird, which builds a scanty nest of small bits of plant stems and wood chips. The cup is lined with softer grasses and leaves. It lays four buff-coloured eggs, camouflaged with brown blotches. During the breeding season it is found near water.

Most migrate south in the autumn; a few, however, spend the winter around Vancouver.

BLACK TURNSTONE
Arenaria melanocephala
smaller than robin-sized

STRIKING IS THE BEST TERM to describe this stocky shorebird. In breeding plumage it is generally all black except for a snow-white belly. The non-breeding and winter plumage is a more subdued brown-black in colour. In flight the wings and body flash an intricate and contrasting black-and-white pattern, undoubtedly making it easier for stragglers to stay with the flock. The bird's rattling call, especially when flying, also helps to keep the flock together and certainly lets you know it is near.

The Black Turnstone is an uncommon visitor to Vancouver's rocky shores and pebble beaches. Some may be found at Stanley Park and near the tips of rocky jetties.

It is most common in Vancouver from October through February. Once the birds arrive in the autumn they are faithful to favoured wintering locations and do not wander far before they leave again in the spring.

COMMON SNIPE
Gallinago gallinago
larger than robin-sized

ONE OF THE MORE WIDESPREAD SHOREBIRDS, the Common Snipe is secretive and solitary and is not often seen in the open. It is a beautifully marked bird, with the upper parts a mixture of different hues of brown on buff. The underparts are white and the tail is a bright red-brown. The head is striped and the bill proportionately very long. Like most shorebirds, it has long legs which enable it to wade in water to feed.

A snipe sits tight to the ground and the first that one knows of its presence is often the sharp *skipe* call, as it zig-zags away at high speed. You may get wet feet searching for this bird because it frequents damp, marshy places around the city.

Like some ground-nesting birds, it will put on an elaborate decoy display to any predators, including humans, that go near the nest. It feeds on invertebrate animals in the mud, for which it probes with its long sensitive bill. Snipe breed near damp marshy places, among tufts of vegetation. The male has a wonderful display flight: from a considerable height he glides steeply down, fanning his tail — which produces a strange *who-who-who* noise.

59

GULLS

COASTAL BRITISH COLUMBIA is one of the best places in Canada to see gulls. In Vancouver alone, fifteen different kinds may be seen. Some of these are very rare visitors, others are numerous during migration periods and one is an abundant year-round resident. All can be found near saltwater, but some travel inland to larger lakes, cultivated fields, and landfills. A good place to observe gulls is from the ferry on its trip between the mainland and Vancouver Island. The following gulls can all be found regularly in season around the city.

BONAPARTE'S GULL
Larus philadelphia
smaller than crow-sized

LOOK FOR THIS SMALL GULL throughout the year but mostly during migration periods in late April and early May and throughout September. During this period, several thousand can be seen together at one time off the Fraser River delta and in Active Pass. In breeding plumage the entire head, including the bill, is black. Outside the breeding season the head is white with a dark spot behind the eye. Immatures are mottled with brown on the back and sides of the body and all have a narrow black tail band. They are noisy when feeding together on small schooling fishes.

MEW GULL
Larus canus
crow-sized

THIS SMALL GULL is more abundant in some winters than is the resident Glaucous-winged Gull, especially in cultivated fields to the south and east of Vancouver. Adults have a small but solid yellow bill, grey mantle, black wing tips with white patches, and pinkish-yellow legs. The size of body and bill relative to other gulls is the best clue for identifying the greyish-brown young. A few Mew Gulls are present throughout the year but this species is most common from August through March. It does not breed in Vancouver; the nearest site is 60 miles to the east of Harrison Lake. It is seldom found very far offshore and prefers to look for its food in sheltered bays, inlets, lagoons and along tide lines.

CALIFORNIA GULL

Larus californicus
larger than crow-sized

THIS VISITOR from the interior of North America appears in small numbers on mud bays and sand flats, mainly during the last half of April. The main influx occurs in autumn, however, mostly in September. Banding returns have shown that Vancouver's visiting California Gulls originate from Saskatchewan, Alberta, North Dakota, Montana, Wyoming, Idaho and the coastal states south of British Columbia. Around Vancouver, it can be spotted among flocks of gulls almost anywhere. Immatures, as with most species of gull, are difficult to identify without the assistance of a field guide.

Left: Mew Gull
Right: Bonaparte's Gull
Bottom: California Gull

HERRING GULL
Larus argentatus
seagull-sized

THIS LARGE GULL IS FOUND throughout the northern hemisphere. The adult has grey on the back, black wing tips, a yellow bill with an orange spot on the lower mandible, and pink feet. The eye is yellow and mean-looking. The only similar gull is Thayer's Gull which is smaller, and its dark eye somehow gives it a "friendlier" look. Young Herring Gulls, like the young of other gulls, are hard to distinguish, as they take four years to reach adult plumage. Before that they are brown and as each year goes by the become a little more grey and white.

For most people, the Herring Gull is the "sea gull," which is really a misnomer, as it breeds mostly in the interior. In Vancouver, it occurs mainly from mid-August to late April, but a few are present throughout the year. Like many gulls, it has learned to take advantage of the messy behaviour of humans. Anyone who has seen the many different species of gulls at a landfill site will realize what an important part our waste plays in their feeding habits, and how important gulls are at keeping city shores clean of garbage.

THAYER'S GULL
Larus thayeri
smaller than seagull-sized

ADULT THAYER'S GULLS are similar in many respects to the more familiar Herring Gull, but are smaller (medium-sized), with no black showing on the underwing tips and usually with brown instead of yellow eyes. Nesting in the high Arctic, this species visits Vancouver only outside the breeding season. Wintering birds begin arriving in late September, increasing their numbers through December; by mid-February most have left again for the north. Its immature plumages challenge even the experts. Like some other gulls it also frequents garbage dumps but can be found most often along the shoreline, usually with other gulls. The Fraser River delta is the best place to find it although a few can be seen throughout most shores of Vancouver.

GLAUCOUS-WINGED GULL
Larus glaucescens
seagull-sized

THE GLAUCOUS-WINGED GULL is the most common resident gull of coastal British Columbia and is the species you will see most often. The adults have a pure white head, except in winter when it is streaked with brown. In flight the wing tips are grey, not black, as in many other gulls. A close relative, the Western Gull, has a darker back, blacker wing tips, and darker underlining on the wings. The similar-sized Herring Gull has black wing-tips.

In May, it builds its nest, using seaweed, grass and other marine debris. It usually lays three olive-brown eggs, which are mottled with darker brown, and young hatch in early July. In Vancouver, it nests on city buildings, shipyards, barges and offshore islets and breakwaters. About 28,000 pairs breed in British Columbia. This gull, like many others, has adapted well to humans and can be found in large numbers wherever we inadvertantly provide food.

Top: Thayer's Gull
Left: Glaucous-winged Gull
Right: Herring Gull

ROCK DOVE

Columba livia

smaller than crow-sized

MOST PEOPLE CALL THEM PIGEONS. Originally from the Mediterranean regions, they have since been introduced into other parts of the world. Their year-round breeding habits led them to be used as a domesticated source of meat. The species has adapted well to inner city living and the ledges of older buildings provide a good substitute for its more natural habitat of rocky cliffs, from which it gets its name. They also forage in city parks, along seashores, and in cultivated fields.

The birds make a scant nest on a ledge and breed in all months of the year, sometimes raising several broods in a year. The young are fed on "pigeon milk" — a liquid produced in the crop of the adult from predigested food. Pigeons have become pests in most large cities; their excrement builds up on the ledges of the buildings and their sheer numbers are a nuisance. One of the principal predators of the Rock Dove is the Peregrine Falcon, a bird which can be seen from time to time around Vancouver's bridges and grain elevators. Occasionally Barn Owls, Great Horned Owls and Bald Eagles use Rock Doves as food in very cold winters.

BAND-TAILED PIGEON

Columba fasciata

smaller than crow-sized

THIS IS TRULY THE WILD PIGEON of British Columbia. Once confined to the southwest coast it is slowly expanding its range eastward and northward in the province. One of the best places to see this bird is in the environs of Vancouver. It is present throughout the year but is most common from May through September. Look for them among mixed woodlands on golf courses, in city parks, and near the coniferous forests surrounding the city, especially in mountainous areas. In autumn and winter they search out berry-producing trees and shrubs.

Band-tailed Pigeons can be distinguished from the city-dwelling Rock Doves by their bright yellow bills and feet, a white crescent on the back of the neck and a wide grey band on the tip of the tail. Band-tails are also slightly larger than their immigrant cousins and rarely are seen in the centre of the city.

Nests are often frail structures of loosely arranged twigs, appearing at times to be incomplete and unable to hold the two white eggs. Nesting begins in May and the young will fly within six weeks. Large flocks may be found in early September in the regenerating forest lands surrounding the city.

WESTERN SCREECH-OWL
Otus kennicottii
larger than robin-sized

THE OWL THAT IS MOST LIKELY to be seen and heard regularly in and around the city is the small Western Screech-Owl, which spends most of the daytime roosting. It is usually encountered at night when its call, a series of short, low notes which accelerate toward the end, gives away its presence. It calls throughout the year, but mostly during the breeding season from February to June. It is easily identified by its "ear" tufts, located outside and above its eyes.

Western Screech-Owls may be found in parks and other wooded areas, or even in quite densely populated areas provided there are enough large trees for cover and nesting. It lays its eggs in April in tree holes and cavities, often in old woodpecker holes — but it will also use nesting boxes erected in trees. This owl feeds on a wide variety of prey including insects, amphibians, fishes, worms, small mammals and birds. On occasion it will catch and kill prey larger than itself. Like many owls, it uses hearing to locate and catch food, but the prominent "ear" tufts have nothing to do with this: the real ears are located on the sides of the head.

GREAT HORNED OWL
Bubo virginianus
smaller than seagull-sized

THIS OWL IS THE MOST widespread of all owls in North America. However, it is rarely seen by most people, except in a fleeting glimpse as it flies across a highway at night. It is a large bird, up to 65 cm long, and the female is larger than the male. Its ear tufts are much larger and farther apart than those of its smaller relative, the Western Screech-owl. The Great Horned Owl's large size, white throat and barred underparts are good identification features.

Great Horned Owls spend much of the day roosting in trees — usually near the trunks — and they do not seem to be put off by some human disturbance. Look for them in woodlands or isolated clumps of coniferous or deciduous trees. Your chances are best in the university endowment lands, north shore mountains, and pockets of mixed woodlands in the Fraser River delta. They are early nesters, laying their two eggs in late February in an abandoned hawk, crow or eagle nest.

They are powerful hunters and one of the few predators that will kill and eat animals the size of a raccoon. They usually eat a variety of small mammals and birds and swallow all but the larger prey items whole. The bones are regurgitated, wrapped in fur and feathers, as a pellet. Watch for these large pellets; they are a good clue to a roost or nest tree.

SNOWY OWL
Nyctea scandiaca
larger than seagull-sized

MORE SNOWY OWLS HAVE BEEN COUNTED in open, agricultural areas south of Vancouver city than anywhere else in North America. They are only winter visitors and are present every year from about November through March. But numbers vary greatly. In some years, it is a challenge to find a single bird; in others hundreds of birds dot fence posts and beach logs. The all-white body and large size make these owls unmistakable.

It is well known that in its Arctic home the Snowy Owl feeds mainly on small mammals, especially lemmings. It was assumed that when it visited southern areas mammals continued to make up most of its diet, but recent studies in the Fraser River delta have shown that small ducks, shorebirds, and other waterbirds are eaten by Snowy Owls, despite an abundance of small mammals.

SHORT-EARED OWL
Asio flammeus
smaller than crow-sized

AN OWL SEEN FLYING over open grassy places or along the edges of a marsh during the day is most likely a Short-eared Owl out hunting. It is a light, streaky brown and its tiny "ears" are not usually visible, except when seen very close. It flies with a very buoyant wing beat and frequently comes to a quick pause to double-check something it has spotted in the grass. It can be seen at any time of day, but is most often seen at dawn and dusk — it is a good bird to watch for along hedgerows, especially in winter.

The Short-eared Owl is present year-round in the outskirts of the city, but it is seen primarily between November and March. Sometimes flocks of 40 to 100 birds can be found roosting communally on the lee side of dikes on Sea and Iona Islands.

It nests on the ground, often in the open, but also in taller vegetation. Like all owls, its eggs are rounded and white. From three to ten eggs are laid, mostly in April. If mice are abundant, however, eggs may be laid as late as June. The Short-eared Owl feeds almost entirely on field mice which it catches by pouncing on them from close to the ground.

RUFOUS HUMMINGBIRD
Selasphorous rufus
smaller than sparrow-sized

DURING SUMMER, this is the common hummingbird of the city. The species migrates north in the spring to breed in western Canada, and British Columbia is the centre of its breeding range in North America. In the winter it migrates south to Mexico. It is hard to mistake a hummingbird: its small size, very rapid wing beats and bright colours are unique. The male Rufous Hummingbird is bright orange-rufous, with an iridescent throat patch or gorget. The female is whiter below, has a green back, rufous sides and lacks a gorget. It may be found in Vancouver from early March to early October.

Hummingbirds will visit the back yard to feed on flower nectar, and are easily attracted to feeders filled with sugar water. It doesn't matter what colour the feeder solution is, but one half cup of white sugar dissolved in enough hot water to make one full cup of solution will keep them coming back.

Hummingbird nests are wonderful structures. They are less than 4 cm in diameter and made from mosses, lichens and plant down, held together with spider webs. Only two eggs are laid, usually between mid-May and mid-June. These are white and relatively large for the size of the birds. The incubation period is about 16 days and young can first fly when they are 21 days old.

BELTED KINGFISHER
Ceryle alcyon
larger than robin-sized

THIS BIG-HEADED, blue-grey and white bird is a familar sight throughout Vancouver. It dives headlong into the water to catch fish, sometimes from a perch 8 or 9 m high. The male has a blue band across the breast and the female is similar, but with a rufous band below the blue on the breast. Its rattling call is a good clue to its presence.

Belted Kingfishers feed on a variety of aquatic food: fish, frogs, tadpoles, salamanders and insects. To see them, look near open water around the city; they feed in rivers, lakes and ponds, as well as along Vancouver's shoreline and inner harbour. They like to fish from a perch overhanging the water, where they can see their prey moving below. They will frequently hover briefly before plunging bill-first into the water.

Kingfishers make their nests at the end of a burrow excavated in a river bank or sea cliff, like those near Stanley Park. The nest is particularly smelly once the young have hatched and the parents have started bringing fish to the young. Like many hole-nesting birds, their eggs are white. In many parts of Canada, kingfishers must migrate south when freeze-up locks out their food source, but here on the west coast they are resident throughout the year.

RED-BREASTED SAPSUCKER
Sphyrapicus ruber
smaller than robin-sized

IT IS HARD TO MISTAKE these colourful woodpeckers for any other species that occurs around the city. Both sexes have bright red heads and breasts, black backs and wings, a pale cream underside and white wing patches. Like all woodpeckers, they nest in holes that they excavate in tree trunks. They can be seen in woodlands at any time of the year and the neat rows of holes they make in tree bark are a good clue to their presence.

Sapsuckers have evolved an interesting food gathering technique. Instead of boring into wood for insects and their larvae, they make shallow, almost square holes in the soft bark of trees, which then ooze the sap which these woodpeckers feed on. They are able to do this because their tongues are different from those of other woodpeckers. Most woodpeckers have long tongues, with barbs at the end to help them "spear" their prey. The Red-breasted Sapsucker has a shorter tongue, with brush-like bristles at the end to help it lap up sap. They also feed on insects attracted to the sap.

DOWNY WOODPECKER
Picoides pubescens
sparrow-sized

THE SMALLEST OF THE WOODPECKERS that you are likely to see in Vancouver, the Downy Woodpecker is about the same size as a sparrow. This is the most common of the woodpeckers to be seen around the city and can only be confused with the Hairy Woodpecker, which is larger (about the size of a robin) and has a longer and thicker beak. The Downy Woodpecker has black wings mottled with white, a white back and underside and a black and white head. The male has a red patch on the back of his head.

If you want to attract them to a winter feeding station, try putting out suet in a plastic vegetable bag or simply hang it from a small branch. These woodpeckers seem to be very tolerant of people and are quite approachable when they are feeding. They nest in holes in trees, which they excavate with their beaks. During the breeding season, the males "drum" on trees — often using dead branches or power poles — which seem to amplify the sound. The Downy Woodpecker's "drum" sounds rather like a fast and prolonged drum roll. Drumming is a form of advertising territory, rather like singing in songbirds. Downy Woodpeckers also have a call, which is rapid and whinnying in tone.

NORTHERN FLICKER
Colaptes auratus
larger than robin-sized

FOR A LONG TIME, it was thought that Red-shafted and Yellow-shafted Flickers were different species, the former found here, west of the Rockies, and the latter to the east of the Rockies. They are now known to be one species, the Northern Flicker. The phrase "red-shafted" refers to the colour of the feather quills of the flight feathers in the wings. Seen from below, these quills are red in the birds commonly found around the city. Probably the most widely noticed of the woodpeckers in this area, it is relatively large — a little smaller than a jay -- with a brown crown, grey face with a red mustache and a black and brown barred body. Its white rump is evident in flight. Unlike other woodpeckers, flickers are often seen feeding on the ground.

They excavate holes in trees for nesting cavities and these holes are often used by other species in subsequent breeding seasons. Birds such as bluebirds, American Kestrels, European Starlings, swallows and the smaller owls — even squirrels — use them. The holes are made in anything of wood, from dead trees to telephone poles and fence posts. They will even try wood on houses; that, combined with their early morning "drumming" on the noisiest thing they can find, such as a metal downpipe, have made them somewhat infamous.

OLIVE-SIDED FLYCATCHER
Contopus borealis
larger than sparrow-sized

THIS LARGE FLYCATCHER would be easily over-
looked if it were not for its habit of perching
near the tops of trees, and for its very distinctive call — *quick-three-beers* — which, once
heard and recognized, is never forgotten.
It has a typical upright flycatcher posture. The bird is olive-brown above,
with white patches on either side of
the rump, best seen when the bird
flies. The breast has a pale central
line separating the olive sides. The
dark tail is comparatively short.

The Olive-sided Flycatcher is a
summer visitor to the city, mainly
from May through August, and
prefers coniferous woodlands and
moist areas. It usually nests in a
conifer, often high up on the end
of a branch. It is particularly fond
of perching in dead trees, from
where it dashes out to catch
insects. Listen for it in the spring
in mountainous areas on the
north side of Vancouver, or
anywhere large tracts of
mixed woodlands exist
around the city. Stanley
Park and the University
of B.C. endowment lands
are good places to search.

HORNED LARK
Eremophila alpestris
larger than sparrow-sized

THE HORNED LARK is a small bird with brown on its back and wings, and sports a black bib, moustache and forehead. It has two small tufts of black feathers on its head, like horns, which it can raise and lower. It spends most of its time on the ground feeding, and outside the breeding season, is often found in flocks. It nests on the ground in open, grassy places, usually in small depressions. Like most ground-nesting birds, it has very well camouflaged eggs. The last nest to be found in the Vancouver area was at the airport in 1970. Still, the Horned Lark is seen throughout the year and may still breed here.

The Horned Lark looks like a large secretive sparrow because it runs or walks, rather than hops. Most of its time is spent in open places south of the city, such as cultivated fields, beaches and sand dunes, where it searches for food. Numbers fluctuate greatly from year to year but the largest flocks have been seen in February, March, September and December.

VIOLET-GREEN SWALLOW
Tachycineta thalassina
smaller than sparrow-sized

THIS SPECIES LOOKS very much like the Tree Swallow. Unlike its relative, though, the Violet-green Swallow has more white on the face, reaching above the eye, and white on its rump extending to its upper flanks. The Tree Swallow, on the other hand, has a metallic blue rump and back. Both species are among the earliest spring migrants to arrive in Vancouver, the first individuals usually here by late February.

It is possible to attract Violet-green Swallows to your garden with suitable nesting boxes. They will take advantage of any appropriate hole or cavity; this might be a crevice high in a cliff, an old woodpecker hole or a hole in a building. They often nest in loose colonies, so it might be worthwhile to put up several boxes a few metres apart. They are often seen over water, where many swallows congregate to catch emerging aquatic insects. The Violet-green Swallow can be seen in the downtown core and inner harbour, flying erratically as it feeds above the trees and buildings.

BARN SWALLOW
Hirundo rustica
sparrow-sized

THE MOST NOTICEABLE FEATURE of the Barn Swallow is its deeply forked tail, which helps it to manoeuvre in flight while catching insects. Its back is uniformly blue and it has a deep red-brown throat, which fades into a cinnamon coloured breast. It is possible to tell the male and female apart by looking at the length of the tail. The male's tail is noticeably longer than the female's, which is only a little longer than the wings when she is at rest.

As its name suggests, the Barn Swallow is more than willing to associate with humans and their structures. Its preference for nesting in buildings, beneath bridges, and under the eaves of houses makes it a commonly seen swallow around the city, and a bird that we have all come to enjoy. It builds its nest from mud and grass collected from a nearby muddy spot. If a pair of swallows starts to build a nest on your property, try providing a wet patch from which they can collect mud; it is fascinating to watch them at close quarters. This species will some-times raise two broods a year and when this happens, the first brood often helps the parents feed the second brood.

STELLER'S JAY
Cyanocitta stelleri
larger than robin-sized

THIS IS THE PROVINCIAL BIRD of British Columbia and, in Canada, is almost completely confined to this province. Perhaps the most noticeable feature of this very handsome bird is its large crest, which it raises and lowers at will. Steller's Jays are common in the mountains on the north side of the city where there are plenty of coniferous trees. Members of the crow family seem to adapt quickly to humans, and jays are no exception: they have learned to associate people with food, and frequent urban back yards looking for scraps. They can be a little shy at the feeder, but nevertheless, they come readily to food put out for them.

Steller's Jays usually nest in coniferous trees. The nest is substantial, if somewhat untidy, and is constructed with twigs lined with mud, grass and roots. Three to five green-blue eggs, evenly spotted with dark brown, are laid. Jays are aggressive in the defence of their nests and will often drive off all but the most persistent intruders, letting the whole neighborhood know about it. They often drift into the city and residential yards in late autumn and winter, where they move from one feeding station to the next with a noisy *shack-shack-shack.*

Left: Inland Race
Right: Coastal Race

NORTHWESTERN CROW

Corvus caurinus

crow-sized

THIS IS THE CROW of the west coast, and is found only from northern Washington to the Aleutian Islands in Alaska. It is a close relative of the American Crow, which is found throughout most of interior North America; however, it is smaller and has a lower *caw*. The Common Raven is larger, by a third.

Crows are renowned for taking advantage of changing circumstances and they have certainly adapted very well to people. One of the reasons that there are so many of them is because they quickly take advantage of humans' habit of leaving food around. They will pull garbage out of bins, scrounge food from tourists, steal food fed to other birds, and frequent the local landfill. Their abundance in Vancouver, however, and all along the British Columbia coast, is a reflection of the plentiful food supply provided by the intertidal zone. The Northwestern Crow is a shoreline feeder first and foremost.

It constructs a somewhat untidy nest of twigs, lined with grass and strips of bark, usually high in a conifer or boulevard tree. It lays four or five dull green eggs, which are blotched with dark brown, in April. Young leave the nest in June.

COMMON RAVEN

Corvus corax

seagull-sized

THIS IS ONE OF OUR MOST EXCITING birds to watch. It is very clever, always on the move, and has many fascinating social traits. The raven is the largest member of the crow family, and is hard to confuse with any other species. When seen in flight, its tail is diamond-shaped. Its wide variety of calls includes a hoarse croak and sounds that are strangely unlike bird calls, almost bell-like. Not quite as bold around people as crows, ravens are still often seen around the city, particularly along the shore.

Ravens are found throughout most of Canada and in the northern regions of Europe and Asia. Although they nest on the ground in Arctic situations, in Vancouver they nest in very tall trees and on bridges. Raven is featured in many west coast Indian stories and is often depicted in traditional art. One of the most exciting depictions of Raven and his association with people can be seen at the Museum of Anthropology at the University of British Columbia. Ravens take advantage of humans. In Vancouver they work together to tip over garbage cans, steal food from pets, especially dogs, and pilfer corn, right from the cob, as it is growing in the fields. They also raid seabird colonies.

CHESTNUT-BACKED CHICKADEE

Parus rufescens

smaller than sparrow-sized

THE MOST COMMON CHICKADEES in British Columbia are the Chestnut-backed Chickadee and the Black-capped Chickadee (*Parus atricapillus*). Both are abundant residents in Vancouver. The Chestnut-backed Chickadee has a brown cap, unlike the black cap of the Black-capped Chickadee, and has red-brown on its back and sides instead of buff. Chestnut-backed Chickadees are birds of mixed forests, although they are also a common sight in any wooded park or back yard in the city. A popular activity in Stanley Park is to feed peanuts to the chickadees from the palm of your hand. They frequent feeders, and are particularly fond of sunflower seeds and suet.

Normally they nest in tree cavities which they often excavate themselves in very soft wood. They will also use holes of other birds such as Downy Woodpeckers, as well as natural cavities. A birdhouse is good substitute. To ensure that sparrows do not take the box over, make your house with an opening of 32 mm (sparrows need 38 mm). Commercial bird houses may be adapted by gluing pieces of wood with the correctly sized opening over the existing hole.

BUSHTIT
Psaltriparus minimus
smaller than sparrow-sized

THE CHARACTER OF THE HOME reflects the quality of the occupant, and the tiny grey Bushtit sets a fine example. The architecture of its nest is worth a close look. Intricate weaving of fine fibres, spider webs, grasses, mosses and lichens results in what one might mistake for an old gray sock hanging from a bushy shrub. A three-centimetre entrance hole is set high on one side, allowing both parents access, yet retaining total concealment of the five or six tiny white eggs. This little bird, with its long, floppy tail, is a masterful weaver.

From July through February, flocks of 15 to 30 move haltingly through the mixed shrubs and trees, hanging upside down or sideways as they search for insect eggs and larvae. They remain in touch with one another more by sound than by sight, their drab bodies and grey-brown heads blending with the shrubbery. Soft, lisping seeps and twitters are often heard before the birds are seen.

Bushtits are a favourite feeder visitor. Beef suet hanging from a flimsy branch (to frustrate crows and starlings) will result in repeated visits from local families of Bushtits. They crowd onto the fat like a swarm of bees. It is then that one can approach for a close-up view.

RED-BREASTED NUTHATCH
Sitta canadensis
smaller than sparrow-sized

NUTHATCHES HAVE a very distinctive shape and the strange habit of moving head-down as they feed from the upper to the lower parts of a tree. These are probably the best clues to their identification. They may have evolved this feeding strategy to exploit the bark of trees from an angle which increases the likelihood of their finding food that other birds have missed.

Red-breasted Nuthatches are rare nesters within the city. They will, however, come readily to feeders — especially those near Stanley Park and the north shore mountains — where they like sunflower seeds and suet. Usually they are found high up in stands of coniferous trees and mixed woodlands.

Nuthatches nest in holes in trees, which they sometimes excavate themselves, although they also use natural cavities and old woodpecker holes. Red-breasted Nuthatches have an interesting habit of smearing pitch or mud around the entrances to their nest-holes. Why they do this is uncertain, but it may serve to reinforce the entrance against predators such as squirrels and starlings, and by reducing the size of the entrance it may prevent larger birds from getting in.

BEWICK'S WREN
Thryomanes bewickii
smaller than sparrow-sized

THIS IS THE MOST COMMON back yard wren of Vancouver. Typical of all wrens, it often cocks its tail over its back, displaying bold brown and white barring. A distinctive white eye-line and whitish underparts separate this species from its closest relative, the House Wren, which is much rarer but also nests here.

Bewick's Wren can be heard year-round uttering a series of clear, sharp notes, often preceded by a buzzy rasp. When alarmed, it alerts other birds by approaching the intruder and scolding noisily. In fact, an effective way of attracting this and many other species is to "squeak" with a kissing or pishing sound to simulate a bird in distress. With practice you may find yourself surrounded by a group of curious and agitated birds, many of which you had no idea were nearby.

Nest sites selected by this insect-eater are sometimes bizarre and imaginative. Wood piles, old jars or baskets tucked away at the back of a shed, electrical fuse boxes and even abandoned wasps' nests may serve as a secure place to raise young ones. Most often, though, a natural cavity in a tree or a small nest box will be used.

WINTER WREN
Troglodytes troglodytes
smaller than sparrow-sized

MORE OFTEN HEARD THAN SEEN, the Winter Wren has a long explosive song which is out of proportion to the size of the bird. It usually sings its series of musical trills from dense cover. This dark brown bird is small, only 10 cm in length, with a short stubby tail which is often carried cocked over its back. When seen at close quarters, its plumage is beautifully barred, the underside paler than the back. In winter, look and listen for it low down in thick, moist, damp woodlands of the city, the closest being Stanley Park. But watch for it in autumn in the garden, if you have an overgrown corner with thick vegetation.

Its scientific name, *Troglodytes*, is most apt. It means "cave dweller" in Greek and, while nesting, the Winter Wren is just that. The male constructs a number of nests for the female to choose from. Each is an elaborate structure of leaves, mosses, grasses and other plant material in the shape of a ball, with a small entrance hole in the side. The nest is usually tucked away in the roots of an upturned tree or under the bank of a stream.

AMERICAN DIPPER

Cinclus mexicanus

larger than sparrow-sized

THIS IS AN EXCITING BIRD to watch. Looking rather like a large fat wren, it is almost uniformly grey and about the size of a European Starling. It is found exclusively beside fast-flowing streams, so a short excursion from the centre of the city will be necessary. There is an excellent chance of seeing this bird beside the fast-flowing rivers on mountains across the inlet from Vancouver. At times a pair frequents the small streams and lake shores in Stanley Park.

American Dippers feed on small aquatic invertebrates and small fishes. To watch a dipper feeding is fascinating, as they frequently search for food below the surface. They do this by wading or diving into the water and then bobbing underneath, where they remain for some time before popping up again. While under water, they actively seek out their prey while walking along the bottom of the stream. Another characteristic to watch for is their constant bobbing up and down, as if the whole bird were on springs. Dippers are often quite hard to spot; the first indication of their presence is likely to be either their loud bubbling song, or a blur of grey as they fly past on their way up or down the river.

GOLDEN-CROWNED KINGLET
Regulus satrapa
smaller than sparrow-sized

RUBY-CROWNED KINGLET
Regulus calendula
smaller than sparrow-sized

BOTH THE GOLDEN-CROWNED KINGLET and its nearest relative, the Ruby-crowned Kinglet, have two white wing-bars and a habit of nervously flicking their wings as they feed. The best way to tell the two apart is to look for the white eyebrow, striped crown and the light belly on the Golden-crown (left). The Ruby-crown (right) is a more evenly-coloured olive-green all over and has a prominent white eye ring. Its striking red crown (male only) is seen only during courtship and aggression.

The Golden-crowned Kinglet is a resident bird wherever coniferous or mixed woodlands occur. Its voice is a high pitched *tsee-tsee-tsee*, so high that it is outside the hearing range of some people.

The Ruby-crowned Kinglet is an autumn to spring visitor, moving north and inland to breed. March and April are the best months to see it here, in mixed deciduous habitats, often in company with small flocks of Golden-crowns. Its surprisingly loud song of up-slurred whistled phrases is the best clue to its presence.

AMERICAN ROBIN
Turdus migratorius
robin-sized

A ROBIN'S SONG is perhaps the best reminder that spring is starting. This, the best known of city birds, is a good example of how well some creatures adapt to the human environment. The robin is really an open forest bird, found wherever there is suitable woodland with clearings — from the tree limit in the north and south across all of Canada. The cities provide a wonderful habitat with their hedgerows, large trees to nest in and plenty of short grassy areas in which to hunt for earthworms and insect larvae. Berries, apples and small fruits are a favorite winter food.

As early as March, the males sing from house tops, trees and telephone wires to define their territories, and it is not unusual to see two males fighting on the ground in a territorial dispute. The birds nest in trees and in suitable recesses in buildings, where they build a sturdy nest of plant stems and coarse grass lined with mud and fine grass. The eggs are pale blue and it is not unusual to find an eggshell on the ground during the spring or summer. If it is chipped neatly in half around the middle, the egg has probably just hatched and the shell been disposed of by a parent.

VARIED THRUSH

Ixoreus naevius

robin-sized

ONE OF THE MOST EVOCATIVE SOUNDS of nature is the song of a Varied Thrush. Its call is a series of unhurried single notes, each of them slightly higher or lower in pitch than its predecessor. It sounds like a human humming and whistling at the same time. This thrush usually sings from cover or high in a tree, and its song is the best clue to its presence. It is a very retiring bird and not always easy to spot. Persevere, as it is a lovely bird to see, a subtle mixture of blue-grey, black and orange. The black chest-band is diagnostic. It is very much a bird of the forest and it is found throughout most of the province where there is suitable cover.

The best time to see this bird in Vancouver is during the rare cold spells of winter, when snows blanket the surrounding hills. At this time, the birds leave the forest and start to forage in any suitable areas, including residential gardens. They can then be seen in the open more often and may even feed on the ground under a back yard feeder. In summer you must climb into the rainforests on the local mountains to be sure to see this bird.

CEDAR WAXWING
Bombycilla cedrorum
larger than sparrow-sized

THIS HANDSOME BIRD can be seen at any time of the year in and around the city, but is most common from June to October. It has an overall sleek appearance, with a very smooth-looking plumage. Red wax-like extensions of the secondary wing feathers give the bird its name. Cedar Waxwings can be found along the edges of most wooded habitats, whether open forest, city parks and streets, or the back yard. Except during the breeding season when they pair off, waxwings spend most of their time in flocks; towards the end of winter these flocks can become quite large. This is a good strategy against predators, such as the Merlin and Sharp-shinned Hawk: flocking often confuses a predator and gives the individual a better chance to get away. Most important, many eyes are better than a single pair for detecting a predator.

In June, this bird builds its nest out on the branch of a tree or bush. The nest is constructed from a wide variety of materials, depending on what is available—an assortment of plant matter including lichens and roots may be used, along with paper, dog hair, twine and whatever else can be found. They lay blue-grey eggs, which are spotted with black or brown.

EUROPEAN STARLING
Sturnus vulgaris
smaller than robin-sized

THIS STUBBY BLACK BIRD is a familiar sight in the city, a truly urban bird that is here year round. The first starlings were brought to New York from Europe in 1890; they have since spread rapidly and are now common over most of North America. It arrived in British Columbia in 1947.

Starlings are really woodland-edge birds, but they are remarkably adaptable and their principal needs are a supply of suitable nesting holes and plenty of nearby grassy areas in which to feed. They nest in old woodpecker holes or in a broken tree branch, but they are just as much at home under the eaves of a house. They find the well cut grass of back yards, golf courses and city parks to their liking, and they do an immense amount of good, feeding on insect grubs. They also appreciate bird feeders.

Starlings are wonderful mimics and incorporate snatches of other birds' songs into their own, Killdeer calls seeming to be a favourite. They also imitate many city noises, including the squeak of garage doors and dog whistles. Although some starlings fly south in the winter, others stay, and on colder days they often huddle over a chimney to keep warm. At night, they roost together in immense flocks on city buildings, under bridges or among boulevard trees.

CRESTED MYNA
Acridotheres cristatellus
robin-sized

VANCOUVER IS THE ONLY PLACE in North America where this member of the starling family can be found. It was introduced to the city from its native Southeast Asia in 1897. Populations peaked to about 20,000 birds in the late 1920s. Since then numbers have been steadily decreasing, mainly because of competition with its relative, the European Starling. Today only 2,000 to 3,000 birds can be found around Vancouver.

Look for a black, robin-sized bird, with a small crest on its forehead. Bold white wing patches and a white tip to the tail are easily seen when the bird is in flight. Search urban lawns, fast food drive-in restaurants, and in winter keep an eye on bridges such as the Burrard and Cambie Street Bridge, where several hundred roost each evening.

The Crested Myna nests in cavities, especially crevices in buildings, bird boxes, drain pipes and lamp posts. It lays two clutches of eggs each year, from mid-April through June.

ORANGE-CROWNED WARBLER
Vermivora celata
smaller than sparrow-sized

THIS BIRD IS NOTICEABLE by its lack of field characteristics. It is a yellow-green warbler, slightly paler below, and the male's dusky orange crown is almost impossible to see unless the bird is handled or seen at close range in good light. It is a common nesting species in open deciduous woodland and along the woodland edges around the city. Even its call is somewhat indistinct until you have heard it a few times. It is best described as a single, slightly descending trill.

YELLOW WARBLER
Dendroica petechia
smaller than sparrow-sized

THIS BRIGHT YELLOW WARBLER is one of the most common and widely distributed of all the wood warblers in the province. It is as likely to be seen in the city as in the more remote parts of the province, from late April through late September. Breeding males start singing in May, soon after they arrive, to establish breeding territories. It is then, before the trees leaf out, that these birds are most likely to be seen. Later in the season, despite their bright colour, they are much harder to spot as they are higher up in tree canopies in search of insects. The male usually delivers his call — *sweet-sweet-sweet-so-sweet* — while sitting at the top of a small tree or shrub.

The Yellow Warbler nests in shrubby trees and bushes and will often nest in gardens if there is some suitable equivalent habitat. The nest is made of grasses and lined with hair and its four or five eggs, white with brown speckles, are mostly laid in late May.

YELLOW-RUMPED WARBLER
Dendroica coronata
smaller than sparrow-sized

FOR MANY YEARS, the two different colour variations of the Yellow-rumped Warbler were treated as separate species, the Myrtle Warbler of the east and Audubon's Warbler of the west. Today, they are known to be one species. Probably Canada's most

Top: Yellow-rumped Warbler
Middle: Orange-crowned Warbler
Bottom: Yellow Warbler

common warbler, it breeds over most of the country.

Both subspecies can be seen here in the city during migration, although Audubon's race is the common nesting form. Its throat, shoulder and crown are yellow, while the rest of the bird is a patterned mixture of blacks, whites and blue-greys. The throat of the Myrtle Warbler is yellow. Unlike most of our warblers, the Yellow-rumped Warbler will overwinter in small numbers on the west coast, particularly around moist shoreline areas. During the summer months, warblers feed on small insects; during the winter, the Yellow-rumped Warbler will eat small berries.

In May, the birds make a loosely constructed and rather untidy nest of roots, grass, and small twigs, lined with soft material. They normally build their nests in a conifer, a few metres from the ground.

COMMON YELLOWTHROAT
Geothlypis trichas
smaller than sparrow-sized

THE MALE COMMON YELLOWTHROAT is striking, and is easily identified by his broad black "robber's" mask that extends well behind the eyes. The female looks somewhat like the male, but lacks the black mask and brightness of colour. These active birds are found in shrubby areas, almost always near water, and they are most common in cattail beds. Listen for the distinctive call, *witchety-witchety-witchety*. From early April to mid-September, they should be found throughout the Fraser River delta, and in Stanley Park, Burnaby Lake and marshy city parks such as Jericho Beach.

WILSON'S WARBLER
Wilsonia pusilla
smaller than sparrow-sized

WILSON'S WARBLER is one of the more common warblers of this part of British Columbia. It is a strikingly bright yellow on the head, breast and underparts and on the top of the male's head is a small black cap, which can be very hard to see if the bird is above you or is moving about in the vegetation. The bird is common in damp places, in fairly thick vegetation. Look for it around ponds, bogs and along stream banks. On migration in the spring and summer, it can be found almost anywhere, even in back yards. It has been seen in Vancouver from mid-April to early November.

Top: Common Yellowthroat
Bottom: Wilson's Warbler

WESTERN TANAGER
Piranga ludoviciana
larger than sparrow-sized

THIS SUMMER VISITOR to the province is a bird of open forests. In Vancouver it is most common in May during northward migration. It may be found in many of the woodlands around the city, as well as in the larger parks, so long as there are plenty of large mature trees. The male is a very attractive bird, washed in red on the head, with a bright yellow body contrasting with black wings and tail. It has very noticeable yellow wing bars, which can be useful in identifying the bird. The female is much less brightly marked, with an olive back and tail, and a pale yellow underside.

The Western Tanager constructs an untidy nest of twigs and grass, often in a coniferous tree. The young birds look very much like the rather drab female once they have fledged. In the autumn the birds move south to winter in Central America. In Vancouver, they are rarely seen after mid-September.

BLACK-HEADED GROSBEAK

Pheucticus melanocephalus

smaller than robin-sized

GROSBEAKS ARE CHARACTERIZED by their large, powerful beaks. The male Black-headed Grosbeak shows a vastly different plumage than the female. He has a cinnamon-brown breast, and black head, back, wings and tail. The wings have two white bars on them — about the only similarity between the sexes. The female is a much more drab, mottled brown. It visits Vancouver, to breed, from late May to late August.

Grosbeaks tend to be birds of mature deciduous woodlands with plenty of shrubby growth below the trees. Typical habitats would be beside lakes, in older mixed forests and alongside streams and sloughs. They find this sort of habitat near Burnaby Lake and occasionally in larger, more mature back yards. They are also present in Stanley Park and the University of British Columbia endowment lands. They nest in trees or bushes and build an untidy and seemingly badly made nest, in which they lay three or four pale blue eggs spotted with brown. The males share the incubating and have a habit peculiar to grosbeaks of singing on the nest. The warblings are somewhat similar to those of the American Robin, but are more clipped and harsh.

RUFOUS-SIDED TOWHEE
Pipilo erythrophthalmus
smaller than robin-sized

THE DENSE UNDERBRUSH OF GARDENS and woodland edges is the favourite haunt of this colourful ground dweller. The Rufous-sided Towhee is a common resident in Vancouver and is sometimes confused with the American Robin. The source of confusion is the colour of the sides and flanks: rufous red in both cases. But the two are not even closely related, the robin being a thrush and the towhee a large member of the sparrow family. On close inspection, the short, conical bill of the towhee, its black hood extending down to the white breast and belly, and its brick-red eyes are diagnostic.

A stroll through Stanley Park or along edges of woodlands will invariably evoke a questioning note from the Rufous-sided Towhee — a nasal, up-slurred *Wheer?* as if to ask "Who goes there?" The song includes repeated phrases, often ending with a sharp trill.

The nest is usually on the ground, well hidden in the base of a thicket or a garden shrub that has trapped a few of last year's fallen leaves. Eggs are laid in May. Grubs and insects make up most of the diet of young birds, but seeds are important through the winter. This bird is a regular visitor to feeders, preferring to feed on seeds spilled to the ground.

FOX SPARROW

Passerella iliaca

sparrow-sized

THE FOX SPARROW can be told from the Song Sparrow by its uniformly dark head and the lack of streaks on the upper parts. It is a large sparrow, with a dark sooty brown head, back and wings. Its breast is pale, with dark streaking well down to the underside. The song is musical and short, a series of two or three slurred notes followed by a series of shorter, quicker notes. In Vancouver, it is heard only in the spring, just prior to its departure northward to the higher forests to nest.

It is found in thickets and scrubby woodland, and can often be seen in urban areas on land that has been cleared and has a dense regrowth of shrubs and brambles. It often finds its way into the back yard in winter, particularly if there is a suitably neglected area and a feeder full of seeds. It is a variable species, with many different plumages throughout Canada. The subspecies found here on the west coast of British Columbia is very dark, but in the north, the red-brown (fox-coloured) subspecies that gives the sparrow its name, is the common form.

SONG SPARROW
Melospiza melodia
sparrow-sized

PERHAPS THE MOST OBVIOUS FEATURE of the Song Sparrow is its long rounded tail. Even when the bird flies, this is one of its most distinctive features, as is the way the bird pumps its tail in flight. The back and wings are a dark, sooty brown. The head is streaked with grey, and the brown streaking of the breast often forms a dark spot in the centre. The Song Sparrow has a very pleasant song which begins with a series of two or three loud notes that are followed by a buzzy call and a trill; listen for it in the spring and summer.

The Song Sparrow is a bird that inhabits bushy shrubbery on the edges of woodland, irrigation ditches and edges of streams, lakes and beaches away from the heavily urbanized areas of the city. Our gardens can often provide just such a habitat, and Song Sparrows are frequently found in gardens that have thick shrubbery or a neglected corner. They will also make use of hedges, which provide suitable nesting sites. A feeder containing mixed seeds will usually attract a Song Sparrow or two for the winter.

Due to the mild climate of Vancouver, Song Sparrows have a long breeding season. Eggs can be found from mid-April through June.

DARK-EYED JUNCO

Junco hyemalis

sparrow-sized

UNTIL ABOUT FIFTEEN YEARS AGO, the "Oregon Junco" and the "Slate-coloured Junco" were considered two of a number of different species of junco, all of which are now recognized as belonging to the same species, the Dark-eyed Junco. The subspecies vary considerably throughout North America and the form most common here, the "Oregon," is perhaps the most attractive. The male and the female look alike, except that the female lacks the jet black hood of the male and has, instead, a dark grey hood.

These birds are commonly seen in the back yard — particularly during the autumn and winter months. The main influx occurs in late September and early October. They are mainly seen at the edges of bushes hunting for food on the ground, or at a feeder. In the breeding season, they tend to frequent the edges of coniferous woodland, and a well treed back yard makes a good substitute. They build their nests on the ground in early April, usually well concealed in the vegetation, or in suitable holes and hollows on or very near the ground. They lay four or five white, speckled eggs from mid-April to mid-May.

SNOW BUNTING

Plectrophenax nivalis

sparrow-sized

THIS BIRD BREEDS in the high Arctic and visits British Columbia mainly in the winter. In the Vancouver area it occurs mainly from November through February, and is best seen in open, often sandy country on the outskirts of the city. The airport and sewage lagoons near Iona Islands are good places to start your search. This attractive bird is seldom seen around human habitation, but it is well worth looking for. Sometimes early autumn migrants are in their white and black plumage but soon after arrival they turn into whitish birds with buff on the head and rump. There is some black on the back.

Large flocks feed together on the ground as they rush about looking for small seeds. Every few minutes the flock will briefly take to the wing and they then become far more obvious, showing off their striking plumage. They rarely perch in bushes or trees, and will even roost on the ground.

RED-WINGED BLACKBIRD

Agelaius phoeniceus

smaller than robin-sized

THE CALL OF THE RED-WINGED BLACKBIRD in the early spring announces the change of season. The male birds are hard to miss with their bright red wing patches, which they use to warn off males from adjoining territories. The size and intensity of colour of the wing patch and the way the bird uses it during his display is directly related to how successful the male is in attracting a mate, or group of females, which will nest in his territory. The female, by contrast, is far less conspicuous and at first glance would appear to belong to a completely different species. She is a heavily striped, brown bird with a marked buff streak over the eye.

Look for them in wet marshes and other areas beside ponds, lakes and along the banks of slow-moving rivers. Colony sites are very noisy with the distinctive *onk-aa-ree-a* call of the males during their frequent territorial disputes. The rough-grass nests are often built on two or more cattail stalks over water in early May. The birds are present year-round in suitable habitats near the city, but their numbers swell in the spring as more birds arrive from southern wintering grounds. Several birds at Lost Lagoon in Stanley Park will feed from an outstretched hand, as long is it is filled with grain.

NORTHERN ORIOLE
Icterus galbula
smaller than robin-sized

THE NORTHERN ORIOLE is not common around the city, or on the west coast, although it breeds commonly in the south-central part of British Columbia and less regularly out to the west coast, including greater Vancouver. This species differs in colour a great deal between the east and the west of the continent: for a long time it was thought that two species existed, the eastern Baltimore Oriole, and Bullock's Oriole in the west. The male Bullock's is handsome, with an orange body, black bib, crown and tail and black and white wings. By contrast, the female is pale olive. It is hard to spot orioles as they spend a good deal of their time high in the tree canopy. The male's rich flutey song usually gives his presence away long before he is sighted.

Orioles build intriguing hanging nests, which they suspend from a branch. They use a variety of plant materials, which they weave into a very strong and durable construction. The nests remain for some time and are frequently built in poplar or other deciduous trees, where they are visible the following winter. Orioles are unusual in their liking for hairy caterpillars which most birds go out of their way to avoid.

PURPLE FINCH
Carpodacus purpureus
smaller than sparrow-sized

HOUSE FINCH
Carpodacus mexicanus
smaller than sparrow-sized

THE PURPLE FINCH (below) is most commonly seen around the city during the winter months but it is present throughout the year. It is a frequent visitor to bird feeders on the outskirts of the city or in the city proper, where it seeks small seeds which it shells with its relatively large beak. The male has a purple-red head and breast and clear belly, while the female is much less gaudy, with an olive-brown back and streaked head and breast. It also shows a light line above the eye. Like all finches, it has a slightly forked tail, which is particularly noticeable in flight. Its call is a distinctive *pic*.

The House Finch is more common, and is also found in the city year round. The red on the breast, head and rump of the male lacks the purplish tones of the Purple Finch and does not extend to the back. The female is grey with light striping and no light eyeline.

Purple Finches inhabit open areas on the edges of mainly coniferous woodland. They build a nest of roots, grass and small sticks and line it with soft material. The nest is normally in a coniferous tree, but is sometimes located in the garden in a suitably dense hedge. House Finches nest in city parks and gardens, often around the vine-covered buildings in the heart of the city.

RED CROSSBILL
Loxia curvirostra
sparrow-sized

AS THE NAME SUGGESTS, crossbills have a unique beak, with the large upper mandible crossing over the lower mandible. This looks awkward until you see the birds using their beaks to extract the seeds of conifer cones; the perfection of the shape then becomes obvious. The Red Crossbill is a medium-sized finch (16 cm in length). The males have a red head and breast and a red-brown back. The females are yellow and brown and the young are mottled on the breast and head, with a brown back and wings.

This species is highly irregular in its distribution. In some years it is very common in coniferous woodlands around the city, but if it is a poor year for coniferous seed cone production, the birds move elsewhere. The crossbill is unusual in that it breeds at almost any time of the year. The birds move about in loose flocks and the *jip-jip* calls and the remains of cones on the ground are good indications of their presence. Watch also for the White-winged Crossbill, which is rare here on the coast but common in the interior of the province. It looks similar, but has two very obvious white wing bars.

PINE SISKIN
Carduelis pinus
smaller than sparrow-sized

THIS SMALL FINCH is seen in large flocks or small groups. It may even breed in loose colonies. Pine Siskins will often visit a feeder, particularly a hanging feeder, if it is stocked with small seeds. They are the most acrobatic of the finches and, like the chickadees, will feed while upside down on an alder or fir twig. Watch for a pale brown, heavily-streaked finch, with some dull yellow on the wings and tail. This yellow is much more noticeable when the birds fly. Like all finches, the Pine Siskin has a forked tail, also more noticeable in flight.

It has a very distinctive call, a good clue to its presence, which sounds like a slightly harsh *zwee-e-e-e-t?* Birds in a flock give this call frequently. A flock of siskins is very active and moves through the trees quite quickly, looking for food. They are predominantly seed eaters, but they also forage for small insects hidden in crevices in the bark. In the early spring they also feed on buds.

AMERICAN GOLDFINCH
Carduelis tristis
smaller than sparrow-sized

IN THE BREEDING SEASON, the male American Goldfinch is a very handsome bird — a bright sulphur yellow, offset with a black cap, wings and tail. The female is a more subdued olive-yellow and she lacks the black cap. In the winter, the birds look somewhat different, the yellow being replaced by a more unobtrusive brown. The birds still show their black wings and tail and the male especially has a little yellow on the throat.

These are seed-eating birds and if you know the location of a large patch of thistles, you will be almost certain to see goldfinches around the plants in the late summer, as they perch on the tops of the seed heads, feeding on the minute thistle seeds. They prefer open places, with trees nearby. A patch of waste ground around the city, or a neglected field, are suitable habitats. They build a cup-shaped nest in trees, of grass and other plant material, which they line with plant down. Their four to six pale blue eggs are laid mostly in the latter part of June.

EVENING GROSBEAK
Coccothraustes vespertinus
larger than sparrow-sized

MOST COMMONLY SEEN around the city in flocks during the spring, the Evening Grosbeak feeds on moth larvae, other arboreal insects and last year's berries and seeds. However it is not very far away in winter and summer. The movements of the Evening Grosbeak are confusing. Some seem to "disappear" into coniferous or mixed forest, while others may migrate out of the province.

In the autumn, the Evening Grosbeaks start to flock and at this time they enter more populated areas around the city. They are readily tempted to the feeder with sunflowers seeds, which they easily crack open with their large bills. The plumage is elegant: a yellow body, black wings, tail and cap and a brown head and neck. The female is buff-coloured instead of yellow and both sexes show a white wing patch in flight. The female Pine Grosbeak is somewhat similar, but Pine Grosbeaks are rare in Vancouver and have black beaks and legs and lack the broad white wing patch. Listen for the piercing call of the Evening Grosbeak as they communicate to keep the flock together.

HOUSE SPARROW

Passer domesticus

sparrow-sized

WHILE WE OFTEN REGARD SPARROWS as pesky nuisances, they are very much a part of city life. Their noisy song is a series of very monotonous *chirrup*s, memorable only for the enthusiasm with which it is delivered!

Outside the breeding season, House Sparrows are often seen in small flocks in both urban and rural areas. They seem to survive well wherever there is human settlement, even downtown. The species is not native to this continent, but was first introduced in the 1850s, ostensibly to help control insect pests. Since then, it has spread to the whole of the continent south of the 60th parallel.

Sparrows are cavity-nesting birds and their adaptability and ingenuity have allowed them to make good use of buildings. They are especially fond of bird houses and will often take over those put up to attract other species, provided the holes are large enough for them: at least 38 mm in diameter. They start breeding as early as April and often have more than one brood. At some city feeders, particularly the tray type, they often dominate. It is less easy for them to chase other birds away at hanging feeders.

ATTRACTING BIRDS

Getting started at birdwatching need not cost a lot of money. Many people derive a great deal of pleasure by simply putting out household scraps for birds on a homemade feeder, close enough to the window that birds can be seen as they come and go.

It is certainly not necessary to be able to identify all the birds at the feeder to be able to enjoy them, but there is a great sense of satisfaction in being able to tell one species from another. Human nature being what it is, we tend to want to learn.

Most people interested in watching birds use binoculars, as this allows them to identify key characteristics such as plumage, leg colour, and bill shape. Binoculars also allow the user to watch the more timid birds that normally stay at a distance, or remain in the cover of bushes and trees, and allow us to study birds' behaviour. Small details help to build the overall picture of a bird, which helps to identify the species.

Buying binoculars is perhaps the biggest financial outlay the birdwatcher will make, but it is not necessary to spend a great deal of money as there are many inexpensive but good models. Buying binoculars can be confusing, and much has been written about how to choose a pair. The best advice is to ask a birdwatcher or to talk to someone at a local nature centre. Remember that no one pair

An attractive back yard offers many birdwatching opportunities.

will be perfect for every situation — watching birds in woodland requires binoculars with a wide field of view but a reasonably low magnification (8X would be ideal), whereas watching shorebirds in an estuary would require a higher magnification, and a telescope would then be useful. Binoculars tend to get heavy around the neck, and it is a good idea to keep this in mind when selecting the right pair. A wider neck strap certainly helps, but if you have a choice, you will not regret going for the lightest pair that seems to be right for you.

Aside from binoculars, the only other piece of equipment needed is a book that will enable you to identify the birds you see. Armed with a pair of binoculars and a good field guide, you will find a whole new world opening up for you as you take advantage of the many excellent birdwatching sites in and around the city, or enjoy your own back yard birds more.

Soon, you will be taking your binoculars with you on a hike or as you take the dog for a walk in the park — the opportunities for their use are endless.

Birds are easily viewed in their natural habitat through binoculars.

BIRD FEEDERS

Why bother with a bird feeder in your back yard? The great advantage is that by feeding birds on a regular basis, they learn to come to that spot every day and as more birds learn, the numbers of species and individuals increase. Your back yard can become your own bird sanctuary.

Feeders also provide advantages for birds. They are used much more frequently when their natural food sources are less abundant — particularly in the winter months. Here on the west coast, we rarely have spells of harsh weather, but when it does get colder, the birds using the neighbourhood feeders may rely on this food source for survival. Once feeding is started, it should be maintained throughout the winter and particularly during the colder weather. A break in the normal routine could well mean that the birds you have so carefully attracted will move on or, if the weather is unusually bitter, may not survive. Try feeding the birds at the same time each day and you will notice how they quickly adjust to a daily routine. Early morning is best. Better still, provide sufficient food to last two or three days.

There may only be a few birds at the feeder at any one time, but this does not necessarily mean that only a few birds are using the feeder. It can be difficult to recognize individuals, but by banding and watching them as they come back to feeders, it has been shown that birds use feeders for only short periods during the day. Any one feeder may be visited by many individuals throughout the daylight hours as they forage through the neighbourhood. This is normal, particularly in the winter when they must range over a much wider area to find the variety of foods they need to sustain themselves.

When you place a feeder in the garden, don't expect the birds to find it immediately. It often takes a few weeks for numbers to build up, so persevere and be patient.

It is best to position the feeder some distance from the house, as the birds will be wary if they see movement. Find a site that is likely to be attractive to birds: immediately adjacent to dense trees or bushes for instance, rather than in the centre of the lawn. Immediate escape cover is as important as the food itself. Small birds are innately aware of the danger of avian predators — Cooper's Hawks, Sharp-shinned Hawks and Merlins — and will soon take a liking to a feeder that offers safety as well as good fare.

Bear in mind also that cats can be a real threat, so make it difficult for them by ensuring that the birds have a chance to see them. Avoid positioning your feeder right beside a suitable hiding place, such as a low bush, and make sure that it is high enough to

Steller's Jays feeding at a tray feeder.

Chestnut-backed chickadees at a seed dispenser.

117

be out of reach of the agile cat — which can leap as high as two metres. A large circle of page wire under the feeder will soon dissuade the neighbour's Tabby.

There are countless designs for bird feeders, but essentially they all do exactly the same job: they dispense food that birds will eat in a convenient and hygienic manner. Depending on the type of birds one wishes to attract, there are four basic designs:

- hanging seed dispensers for bird seed
- tray feeders for mixed bird foods
- suet feeders
- hummingbird feeders

Hanging Seed Dispensers

These come in many different designs, but if you bear a few points in mind it is easy to select the right one.

The feeder should be large enough to hold a good supply of seeds; otherwise, you will be forever refilling it. The ease with which the feeder can be filled is also important. Birds will eat most during the coldest periods, so you'll need a feeder that is easy to open and close on a cold day.

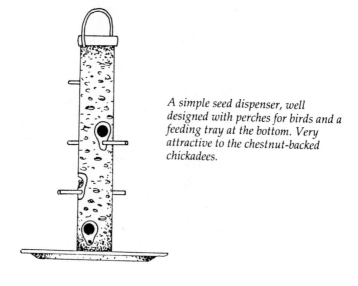

A simple seed dispenser, well designed with perches for birds and a feeding tray at the bottom. Very attractive to the chestnut-backed chickadees.

Left: A larger seed dispenser that holds more food and has larger openings to allow bigger birds to use it.
Right: A seed hopper with a plastic dome that keeps off squirrels and larger birds. It has good seed capability and is ideal for smaller birds.

All feeders should be cleaned regularly so they should be easy to take apart. The seed should be protected from the rain and snow. Clear plastic seed containers are the best — they clean easily, are reasonably strong, allow you to see when they need refilling, and allow the birds to see what is inside them.

There are many commercial seed mixtures available for hanging feeders, but a surprising number of birds seem to prefer sunflower seeds: if you put up two feeders, one with a mixture and one with sunflower seeds, you will be able to observe the preferences yourself.

A tray-type feeder with a hopper that has see-through side for easy checking of food levels.

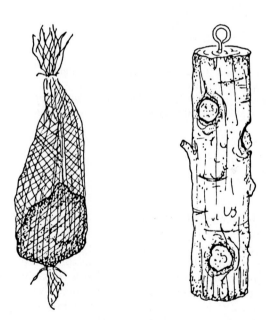

Left: The simplest of all suet dispensers: an old onion bag, easily replaceable. Right: A more natural type of suet dispenser: an old log with holes drilled in it and stuffed with suet.

Tray Feeders

This type of feeder can be designed to attract many different types of birds, from seed eaters to those that forage on the ground. Some tray feeders have a hopper, with the tray immediately below to catch the seed and provide a feeding area. These work well, but have some disadvantages. There is never enough room for all the birds to feed without overcrowding, and so the more dominant species and individuals tend to drive others away. It is also quite difficult to see the birds at the feeder. The more timid ones tend to feed on the side furthest from your sight —a problem which can be overcome if you arrange to have only one outlet.

Perhaps the best type of tray feeders are those that are nothing more than a large tray, onto which seed and other scraps are spread. It should have a lip to stop too much food from spilling or blowing onto the ground. But don't worry about the spillage; you will find that many species prefer to feed on the ground under the feeder. Position this type of feeder near some dense tree or shrub cover. And again, a temporary wire fence with at least 10 cm mesh will keep the cat from lunging directly under the feeder, yet will allow casual access even for large birds.

Suet Feeders

You can get beef suet from the meat counter at the supermarket and birds such as woodpeckers, chickadees and Bushtits love it. It is a good high-energy food for birds in cold weather and is easy to feed as it comes in a lump, lasts a while, and can be simply suspended in an old onion bag or from a string. Other types of suet feeders can be made using wire mesh: the plastic-coated type is best, as birds can damage themselves on normal metal mesh especially in cold weather. If you have the tools, bore holes in a short log and push suet into the holes, then hang this up.

Hummingbird Feeders

It is possible to attract hummingbirds into your garden with a colourful variety of flowers, but a good hummingbird feeder is one of the best ways to keep them coming back. When buying a feeder, look closely at the seals that keep the fluid in the container and choose one that looks well made. Most of them work, but the cheaper ones don't last long and frequently drip. This attracts wasps, bees and ants and leaves the feeder empty in short order. A hummingbird feeder should have some red on it, as this helps to attract the birds. You can make your own feeding fluid by dissolving two to three parts of white sugar in one to three parts of near-boiling water. Experiment and see what concentration seems to be preferred. There is no need to add red dye to the liquid, and never use honey as this ferments readily and may grow a mold that can be fatal to hummingbirds. It is important to clean the feeder frequently. In warm weather, add only a bit of liquid each time and let your feathered visitors consume it before it ferments. Keep the refill jar in the refrigerator.

Because hummingbirds are so small, it is most rewarding to hang the feeder near a window, or on the deck, where the birds quickly become accustomed to people and will allow you to watch at close range.

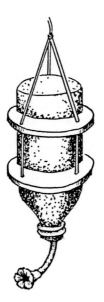

A home-made hummingbird feeder. Use an artificial red flower at the mouth.

Nest Boxes

Different species of birds have evolved to take advantage of different habitats. Each species uses a different feeding strategy and a different nesting strategy. By providing a variety of different types of food at your feeder, it is possible to attract ground-feeding birds and tree-feeding birds, seed eaters, omnivorous birds and even the odd bird of prey. The same is true if one provides a variety of different nesting opportunities. Birds will be attracted to artificial sites during the breeding season. Although some boxes may not be used the first year, they can be relocated next season.

There are many misconceptions about nest boxes. For example, birds don't need a perch on the front of the bird house — a perch is most useful for predators such as starlings that are trying to steal eggs or young. Although you may appreciate rounded corners on a bird house and a well-sanded exterior, birds prefer rough wood and a natural look. At the end of the season, clean the nest box out. This helps to prevent nest parasites from over-wintering, and

A few examples of different styles of nest boxes.

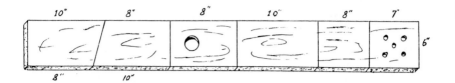

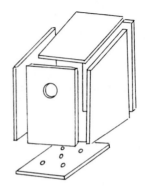

The construction of a nest box
from a plank of wood.

gives birds a vacant box for the following spring. Don't disturb the
house when it's in use as you may cause the adults to desert their
eggs or young.

There are many different designs for nest boxes, but the most
common and often the most effective is a very simple box that can
be made from a single plank of wood. By altering the inside
dimensions, the size of the hole, and the site where the box is
placed, you should be able to attract a variety of different species.

Here are a few basic dimensions for some of the most common
cavity nesting species:

Species	Floor Size	Depth	Hole Diameter	Height above ground
Western Bluebird	13x13 cm	20 cm	38 mm	1-3 m (on post or tree)
Chestnut-backed Chickadee	10x10 cm	23 cm	29 mm	1.5-5 m (in tree)
Downy Woodpecker	10x10 cm	23 cm	32 mm	2-6 m (on tree)
Hairy Woodpecker	15x15 cm	35 cm	38 mm	4-6 m (on tree)
House Finch	15x15 cm	15 cm	50 mm	2-4 m (on tree)
House Sparrow	10x10 cm	23 cm	38 mm	1-4 m (on house or tree)
Red-breasted Nuthatch	10x10 cm	23 cm	32 mm	2-6 m (on tree)
Northern Saw-whet Owl	15x15 cm	28 cm	64 mm	4-7 m (on tree)
Western Screech-owl	20x20 cm	35 cm	76 mm	3-10 m (on tree)
European Starling	15x15 cm	40 cm	50 mm	3-8 m (on house or tree)
Violet-green & Tree Swallows	13x13 cm	15 cm	38 mm	3-5 m (on tree or post)
Wood Duck	27x27 cm	60 cm	76 mm	3-7 m (near water)

There are some basic rules to be kept in mind. If the nest box is exposed to full sunlight during the hottest part of the day, the nestlings may die from heat exhaustion, so choose a shaded area, or the northeast side of an exposed tree, post or building. If the box is on a wall, the same will apply — so choose a spot that is shaded by a tree or a climbing plant. Keep the box level or tilted slightly down so that the hole is not exposed to rain. Avoid trees that cats like to climb, or put on an anti-cat barrier at the bottom: an inverted wire cone fixed to the tree about 1 1/2 metres above the ground usually suffices. There is nothing more upsetting than having the family cat bring you a present of the young birds that you have been watching.

Try to put the nest box in a position that looks as natural as possible and emulates a natural cavity. For your own pleasure, situate it where you can see what is going on from some convenient vantage point.

Nest box placement.

A BIRD GARDEN

Food, shelter and water are the necessities for all birds at all seasons. A simple bird feeder will bring a variety of seed-eating birds to the garden, but there is little chance of luring insect-eating birds without an appealing environment for them. Even some of the seed-eating species are very shy at the feeder and to attract these birds it is necessary to "think natural" and create some attractive mini-habitats.

It is possible to determine the types of birds that will come to your garden by providing the sort of surroundings that give them shelter, nesting opportunities and food. Flycatchers and other insect-eating birds will be attracted in spring and summer to flower gardens where insects are likely to be abundant. Seed-eating birds will find both shelter and food in the wilder sections of a back yard, where shrubs and weeds combine to provide dense cover and year-round access to food in the form of seeds. A varied garden plot will lure birds where a flawless lawn will not, and a mix of shrubs and taller trees will attract a far greater variety and abundance of birds than a hedge of uniform trees or shrubs. It is not only berry bushes and fruit trees that provide food; seeds, insects feeding on plants, and water are at least as likely to entice birds.

Birds are also attracted to gardens where there is plenty of shelter in which to rest during the day, or to roost at night, where

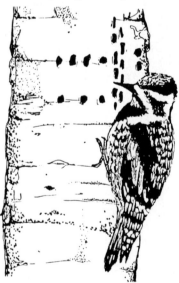

Sapsucker drilling holes on an alder tree trunk for sap.

they can escape from the hottest weather in the summer, and find some protection in the winter. Gardens with mature trees and plenty of shrub cover will be attractive. Some birds also appreciate an area of longer grass and if it is possible to keep an area of the garden as "wild" as you can, it will attract all sorts of creatures, not just birds.

Planting to Attract Birds

Berry Bushes Native shrubs are a principal food source for birds in the wild and will prove a major attraction for birds in the city as well. Although it is possible to transplant shrubs from the wild, this may not be a very conservation-minded practice, unless it is done with care and forethought and with species whose abundance is not an issue. Obviously, if you can get to an area before a developer clears the vegetation, you will not be doing any damage. However, this is not always easy to do and an obvious way to get around the problem is to grow plants from cuttings or seeds. If this does not appeal to you, then try some of the better garden centres, many of which offer a complete range of native shrubs and trees, along with a great deal of good advice.

Among those shrubs that are practical to transplant, and attractive to birds, are blue elderberry and red elderberry, Oregon grape, black twinberry, salal, Indian plum, squashberry, snowberry, thimbleberry, salmonberry, huckleberry, black raspberry, wild rose, flowering currant, gooseberry and blackberry.

Domestic varieties of some of these berry bushes can be obtained from the larger nurseries and garden centres. They may also supply you with a host of other choices in shrubs that birds find equally attractive, including cotoneaster, pyracantha, honeysuckle, raspberry, red and black currant and viburnums.

Trees Fruit trees and bushes sometimes provide an unwelcome attraction to birds, as anyone who grows fruit will know. However, some trees produce fruit that is very attractive to birds, but of little or no value to humans. Trees such as the mountain ash are good berry producers and will be visited by American Robins, Cedar Waxwings and other species. Other trees, such as the black hawthorn, Pacific crabapple, bitter cherry, cascara and Pacific dogwood are worth planting and cultivating as they may well be visited throughout the winter, or as long as the fruits remain on the trees. Watching the birds search out the fruits will provide you with a good deal of enjoyment.

Starling resting on a fence post.

Water Birds need water throughout the year. A bird bath that is kept unfrozen in the coldest weather will attract many birds. During the summer months, a bird bath can become a busy place. Birds like to bathe more in the summer, and bird baths can provide endless pleasure for both the birds and the birdwatcher.

Choose or build a bird bath that is not too deep (no more than 7 cm), shelves gradually and is finished in a rough texture so that it is easy for birds to grip. Birds get engrossed in drinking and bathing and when they have wet feathers, they don't fly quite so well. Therefore, if the bath is on or near ground level, make sure that it is situated well away from bushes, so that cats can not approach the bath unseen.

You can keep the water in your bird bath unfrozen during the coldest winters with a small heater available on the market, and you can make the bath particularly attractive to birds in summer by creating a trickly flow or spray of water with a small electric pump.

SEASONS OF BIRDWATCHING

Spring

Spring comes early to the west coast with no marked change in seasonal conditions. The first sign of spring is often the increase in the number of ducks on the estuaries and lakes, as birds from the south push north, waiting for the break-up of the ice on their inland breeding sites. The first of the ducks to arrive may be the elegant Northern Pintail, which begin to come north in February. Also arriving in February are the earliest swallows, the Violet-green and Tree Swallows.

This is the time of year when bird-song also begins and many birds that have overwintered suddenly become more noticeable as they begin to establish breeding territories. Some species, such as Great Horned Owls and Western Screech-owls, which are here throughout the year, are best found at this time of the year. Take a walk through one of the forested parks around the city at dusk or before dawn and you may well be rewarded by hearing them.

The increase in bird activity is the prelude to the breeding season and you will notice that many of the birds are actively involved in courtship behaviour. Waterfowl go through many of their breeding displays on the water, and some are very attractive to watch, particularly those of the goldeneyes and Bufflehead. Like the Mallard, the Bufflehead's courtship is far from sedate, with the female frequently being pursued none too gallantly by many males.

Spring is also the time of year when it is easiest to see birds in and around the city. Not only are the numbers and variety of birds swelled by the migrants that are arriving to breed, or passing through on their way to their northern breeding grounds, but the lack of leaves on the deciduous trees makes seeing them much easier. Without doubt, early May is the best time of year to watch for warblers. Later in the year, not only will it be harder to spot them, but the young "look-alike" birds will confuse even the most experienced birder.

Perhaps the most thrilling of the spring sights and sounds, though, are the few skeins of geese that pass high over the city on their flight northward. Canada Geese and occasionally White-fronted and Snow Geese may be seen.

Summer

Summer is the breeding season for most birds and this means a great deal of singing, displaying and nest-building. Once the serious business of incubating the eggs and feeding the young starts, birds become less noticeable and once more secretive. It can be an advantage for a bird to announce its presence when trying to attract a mate or establish a territory, but once eggs are laid and the young hatch, there is a greater need to incubate and feed young birds, and remain undetected by predators.

For those who have put up nest boxes or have the good fortune to have their trees or gardens selected as nesting sites, this time can be great fun. There is something enormously satisfying about witnessing the breeding cycle of birds. From start to finish, it may take a chickadee only about a month to find a mate, build a nest, lay eggs, hatch them and feed their young to the point of fledging. If they happen to use a nest box that you have put up for them, this becomes a very personal experience and the sense of thrill when the young birds fly comes as quite a surprise.

Ducks moult at this time of year and both the male and the females look very much alike for a while. When ducks are moulting, it is known as the "eclipse" plumage; some species can look very different and even the common male Mallard may require more than one look before identification is possible. Birds moult at this time of year to renew their flight feathers before their fall migration, while there is still an abundance of summer food available.

The display posture of a male red-winged blackbird during the mating season.

Autumn

As early as August, birds that have completed their breeding cycle for the year will start migrating south. Birds that breed in the Arctic must complete their breeding as quickly as possible because, by late summer, food sources are already less abundant and colder weather has begun. As young birds fledge, the birds leave their breeding grounds and begin to arrive along our coast. Watch for the increase in numbers of shorebirds and waterfowl now. Estuaries, bays and lakes with muddy shores are particularly good places to visit at this time of year.

Autumn is also the time of year when warblers and many of the other small birds can be frustratingly hard to identify, as the young birds and the moulting adults do not always look the way they ought to according to the books!

Shorter daylight hours and an end to the breeding cycle can often induce some birds — particularly the crows and starlings — to begin their communal roosting behaviour. Each evening large flights of Northwestern Crows stream over the residential areas on their way to safe night roosts on nearby off-shore islands. Similarly, European Starlings begin to arrive at their night roosts as darkness approaches. Large flocks can be seen in the downtown area as they wheel and circle over their safe havens.

Autumn is the best time to watch out for rarer birds, so be prepared to take a close look at anything that seems odd or unusual. Migrants, especially juveniles, can easily take the wrong turn, and here on the west coast it is possible to get Eurasian birds migrating down the wrong side of the Pacific seaboard. Check every bird in a flock of ducks or shorebirds and look for colours or features that are different from the majority's. Then check your field guide to see if you have found a rarity.

Winter

Here on the west coast, we can look forward to many more species of birds remaining throughout the winter months than is possible in other parts of Canada. The variety of waterfowl and seabirds during the winter can be a source of many hours of fruitful birdwatching. Many bird species overwinter in this coastal area for exactly the same reason that we enjoy living here — the winter temperatures are relatively warm and there is little snow. This means that certain birds do not need to fly south to find a suitable place to over-winter. Birds normally migrate to avoid the harsh weather which makes feeding difficult and birds such as the warblers that rely on a ready source of small insects — which become less available, even in our gentle winters — must leave most Canadian areas.

Early winter is the time of year when feeders work particularly well in attracting birds into the garden. Once you have attracted a few, more will tend to show up and linger on — perhaps even through the winter — because there is safety in numbers. Many birds react swiftly to the danger signals of other species. Although some of the smaller birds will have migrated south, some of the woodland species can be easier to see at this time of year, as there are fewer leaves on the deciduous trees and bushes. Look out for woodpeckers, which always seem more visible in the winter.

This is a good time of year to check your nest boxes, to ensure that they are not broken and to clean them. Put a little dry grass or a few wood shavings in the bottom; this allows air to circulate and helps to make them more attractive to birds in the spring.

KEEPING BIRD NOTES

Now that you have birds coming to the feeder and birds nesting in the bird boxes, why not keep a record of which birds you see in your yard, when, how many and how often? Keeping records is the only way of noting changes and will provide you with many hours of pleasure. A daily or weekly checklist of sightings will tell you a great deal about your avian visitors. It will furnish a record of how numbers change throughout the seasons and from year to year, and of specific migration times of many species. You will soon know just when to expect your first Rufous Hummingbird of the spring, or the first Golden-crowned Sparrow of the autumn.

If you spend time hiking through nearby natural areas or parks, your observations will help you to remember what you saw and when. These observations will tell you what birds were common in which years and what parts of the area were particularly good for various species. As well as being of interest to you, you may be able to make an important contribution to local knowledge by helping ornithologists understand how numbers of birds in your area are changing. This sort of information is often not available when it is needed, and may also help to protect your favorite birding spot, should it be threatened with development. The Royal British Columbia Museum and provincial Wildlife Branch appreciate receiving sight-record cards documenting your bird observations, especially those of our less common species.

Keeping good records may allow you to convince the experts that you have seen a particularly rare bird, or may help you

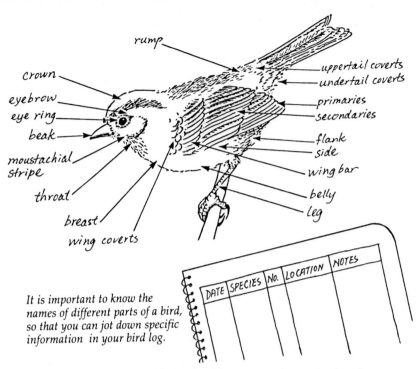

It is important to know the names of different parts of a bird, so that you can jot down specific information in your bird log.

describe a problem species to an expert. Try to record a clear image of what the bird looked like — a simple line sketch is ideal, and it really doesn't matter how artistic it is! Include as much information as you can about the bird, its plumage characteristics, its bill, leg colour, sounds, and what behaviour the bird exhibited.

You might also want to keep a bird log. This would include the species you saw, how many, where and when (see diagram).

Keep your records in a notebook to avoid losing them. If you intend to take your notebook on hikes, choose one that has a soft waterproof cover; this will allow you to stuff it into a pocket or your pack and it will not disintegrate in the rain. A useful tip: pencils are easier than pens to sketch with, and they write more easily on damp paper.

Another good way to learn more about birds is to join your local natural history or bird society. You will meet many knowledgeable people who will be pleased to teach you what they know about birds and the best places to see them in various areas. Many organizations run field trips to some of the good birdwatching spots and provide the benefit of an expert to help with identification problems.

Good birding!

CHECKLIST OF
COMMON VANCOUVER BIRDS
(1988 EDITION)

Area Covered:

Greater Vancouver and vicinity from International Boundary (but including Point Roberts, Washington) north to 49°35'N, west to Georgia Strait and Howe Sound (including islands in Howe Sound), east to 122°30'W (260th Street in Langley and Maple Ridge), but including all of Golden Ears Park.

Explanation of Symbols:

Abundance or frequency of occurrence in suitable habitat:

a = abundant; very large numbers (generally 100 or more per day)

c = common; large numbers (25 to 100 per day)

fc = fairly common; moderate numbers (5 to 25 per day)

u = uncommon; small numbers (1 to 5 per day), but at least 10 records per season; easily missed in an average day's birding

ra = rare; regular, 1 to 10 records per season, usually seen singly or in very small numbers

ca = casual; 3 to many records, but seen on average less than once a year; somewhat out of normal range

acc = accidental; 1 to 2 records; usually far outside normal range

Seasonal Status:

R = resident, present all year round

W = winter resident, including fall arrival and spring departure

Sp = spring transient (generally March through early June)

S = summer resident, including spring arrival and fall departure

F = fall transient (generally July through November)

T = transient in spring and fall

Other Symbols:

* = species known to have bred in the checklist area

sr = sight record; indicates casual and accidental species for which no specimens, photos, or tape recordings exist for the area, but for which acceptable field descriptions are on file.

Red-throated Loon	caS, fcW, cT	Black Scoter	raS, cW
Pacific Loon	raS, uW, cT	Surf Scoter	fcS, aW
Common Loon	uS, fcW, cT	White-winged Scoter	uS, cW
Yellow-billed Loon	caS, raW	Common Goldeneye	raS, cW
		Barrow's Goldeneye	raS, aW
*Pied-billed Grebe	fcR	Bufflehead	raS, cW
Horned Grebe	raS, cW	*Hooded Merganser	raS, fcW
Red-necked Grebe	raS, fcW	*Common Merganser	uS, cW
Eared Grebe	caS, uW	Red-breasted Merganser	caS, cW
*Western Grebe	fcS, aW	*Ruddy Duck	raS, cW
*Double Crested Cormorant	fcS, cW	Turkey Vulture	raS, uF, caW
Brandt's Cormorant	caS, uW		
*Pelagic Cormorant	fcR	*Osprey	uS, caW
		*Bald Eagle	uS, fcW
*American Bittern	uR	*Northern Harrier	uS, cW
*Great Blue Heron	cR	*Sharp-shinned Hawk	raS, uW
Cattle Egret	caSp, raW	*Cooper's Hawk	uR
*Green-backed Heron	uS, caW	Northern Goshawk	caS, raW
*Black-crowned Night-Heron	raR	*Red-tailed hawk	fcS, cW
		Rough-legged Hawk	fcW
Tundra Swan	uW	*Golden Eagle	raR
Trumpeter Swan	fcW		
Greater White-fronted Goose	caS, uT, raW	*American Kestrel	raS, uT, raW
Snow Goose	caS, aW	*Merlin	caS, uW
Brant	raS, cSp, uW	Peregrine Falcon	raS, uW
*Canada Goose	aR	Gyrfalcon	raW
*Wood Duck	fcR	*Ring-necked Pheasant	fcR
*Green-winged Teal	uS, aW	*Blue Grouse	fcR
*Mallard	cS, aW	*Ruffed Grouse	uR
*Northern Pintail	uS, aW	*California Quail	raR
*Blue-winged Teal	fcS		
*Cinnamon Teal	cS, caW	*Virginia Rail	fcR
*Northern Shoveler	uS, cT, fcW	*Sora	fcS, caW
*Gadwall	cs, fcW	*American Coot	uS, cW
Eurasian Wigeon	uW		
*American Wigeon	uS, aW	*Sandhill Crane	raR
Canvasback	raS, cW		
Redhead	raR	Black-bellied Plover	uS, aT, cW
Ring-necked Duck	raS, uW	Lesser Golden Plover	caS, uT, accW
Tufted Duck	caS, raW	*Semipalmated Plover	raS, fcSp, cF, caW
Greater Scaup	uS,aW	*Killdeer	cS, fcW
Lesser Scaup	uS,cW		
*Harlequin Duck	uS, fcW	*Black Oystercatcher	raR
Oldsquaw	raS, fcW		

Greater Yellowlegs	raS, fcT, raW	Common Tern	raS, cT
Lesser Yellowlegs	raS, uSp cf, raW	Arctic Tern	caSp, raF
Solitary Sandpiper	raT	*Black Tern	raS
Willet	raS, caW		
Wandering Tattler	caSp, raF	Common Murre	raS, fcW
*Spotted Sandpiper	fcS, raW	*Pigeon Guillemot	fcS, uW
Whimbrel	uS, fcSp, caW	*Marbled Murrelet	fcR
Long-billed Curlew	caS, raT, caW	Ancient Murrelet	uW
Hudsonian Godwit	caS, accSp, raF	Rhinoceros Auklet	raS, caW
Marbled Godwit	raT		
Ruddy Turnstone	raT, caW	*Rock Dove	aR
Black Turnstone	fcW	*Band-tailed Pigeon	cS, uW
Surfbird	uW	*Mourning Dove	uR
Red Knot	caS, uT, caW		
Sanderling	raS, cW	*Common Barn Owl	uR
Semipalmated Sandpiper	caS, raSp, fcF		
Western Sandpiper	cS, aT, raW	*Western Screech-Owl	uR
Least Sandpiper	uS, cT, caW	*Great Horned Owl	uR
Baird's Sandpiper	raSp, fcF	Snowy Owl	uW
Pectoral Sandpiper	raSp, cF	*Northern Pygmy-Owl	raR
Sharp-tailed Sandpiper	uF	Spotted Owl	raR
Rock Sandpiper	raW	*Barred Owl	uR
Dunlin	raS, aW	*Long-eared Owl	raR
Stilt Sandpiper	caSp, raF	*Short-eared Owl	raS, uW
Buff-breasted Sandpiper	raF	*Northern Saw-whet Owl	uR
Ruff	caSp&S, raF		
Short-billed Dowitcher	raS, cSp, uF	*Common Nighthawk	raS
Long-billed Dowitcher	uS, fcSp, aF, uW		
*Common Snipe	uS, fcW	Black Swift	fcS
*Wilson's Pharalope	uS	*Vaux's Swift	fcS
Red-necked Pharalope	caS, raSp, uF		
		Anna's Hummingbird	raS, uW
Pomarine Jaeger	acc Sp&S, raF	Calliope Hummingbird	raSp
Parasitic Jaeger	raSp, uF	*Rufous Hummingbird	rcS, cSp
Franklin's Gull	caS, uF, CaW		
Bonaparte's Gull	cS, aT, raW	*Belted Kingfisher	uR
Heermann's Gull	caSp, fcF		
Mew Gull	uS, aW	*Lewis' Woodpecker	raT, caW
Ring-billed Gull	cS, aF, fcW	*Red-breasted Sapsucker	uR
California Gull	fcR, cT	*Downy Woodpecker	fcR
Herring Gull	caS, uW	*Hairy Woodpecker	uR
Thayer's Gull	caS, cW	Three-toed Woodpecker	raR
Western Gull	caS, raW	*Northern Flicker	fcR
*Glaucous-winged Gull	aR	*Pileated Woodpecker	uR
Glaucous Gull	raW		
Caspian Tern	fcS, accW	*Olive-sided Flycatcher	fcS

*Western Wood-Pewee	uS, fcT	*American Robin	aS, cW
*Willow Flycatcher	fcS	*Varied Thrush	fcS, cW
*Hammond's Flycatcher	fcS		
*Western Flycatcher	fcS	*Gray Catbird	raS
Say's Phoebe	raT		
Ash-throated Flycatcher	accS, raF	*Water Pipit	raS, cT, uW
Western Kingbird	raSp&S, caF		
*Eastern Kingbird	uS	*Bohemian Waxwing	raS, uW
		*Cedar Waxwing	cS, uW
*Horned Lark	raR		
		Northern Shrike	uW
*Tree Swallow	cS, accW		
*Violet-green Swallow	cS, aSp	*European Starling	aR
*Northern Rough-winged Swallow	fcS	*Crested Myna	uR
Bank Swallow	raSp, uF		
*Cliff Swallow	cS	*Solitary Vireo	fcS
*Barn Swallow	aS, caW	*Hutton's Vireo	uR
		*Warbling Vireo	fcS
*Gray Jay	uR	*Red-eyed Vireo	fcS
*Stellar's Jay	fcR		
*Northwestern Crow	aR	*Orange-crowned Warbler	cS, caW
*Common Raven	fcR	Nashville Warbler	raT
		*Yellow Warbler	cS
*Black-capped Chickadee	aR	*Yellow-rumped Warbler	uS, aT, uW
Mountain Chickadee	raR	*Black-throated Gray Warbler	fcS
*Chestnut-backed Chickadee	aR	*Townsend's Warbler	cS, caW
		Northern Waterthrush	raF, accSp&W
*Bushtit	cR	*MacGillivray's Warbler	fcS
		*Common Yellowthroat	cS, caW
*Red-breasted Nuthatch	uR	*Wilson's Warbler	fcS, caW
*Brown Creeper	uR	*Western Tanager	fcS
*Bewick's Wren	fcR	*Black-headed Grosbeak	fcS
*House Wren	raS	*Lazuli Bunting	raS
*Winter Wren	cR		
*Marsh Wren	cR	*Rufous-sided Towhee	cR
		American Tree Sparrow	raW
*American Dipper	raR	*Chipping Sparrow	caS, raT, accW
		*Savannah Sparrow	cS, aT, raW
*Golden-crowned Kinglet	aR	Fox Sparrow	cW
*Ruby-crowned Kinglet	raS, cT, fcW	*Song Sparrow	aR
Mountain Bluebird	raT, caW	Lincoln's Sparrow	caS, uSp, fcF, raW
*Townsend's Solitaire	uSp, raR	White-throated Sparrow	raW
*Swainson's Thrush	aS, accW	*Golden-crowned Sparrow	caS, cT, fcW
*Hermit Thrush	fcS, raW	*White-crowned Sparrow	cR, aT

Harris' Sparrow	raW
*Dark-eyed Junco	fcS, aW
Lapland Longspur	uT, raW
Snow Bunting	uW
*Red-winged Blackbird	cR
*Western Meadowlark	raS, uW
*Yellow-headed Blackbird	uS, caW
Rusty Blackbird	raF, caW&Sp
*Brewer's Blackbird	cS, aW
*Brown-headed Cowbird	cS, uW
*Northern Oriole	uS
Rosy Finch	raW
Pine Grosbeak	caS, raW
*Purple Finch	fcR
*House Finch	cR
Red Crossbill	fcR
White-winged Crossbill	raR
Common Redpoll	raW
*Pine Siskin	cS, aW
*American Goldfinch	cS, fcW
*Evening Grosbeak	fcS, cW
*House Sparrow	aR

Total 253 species

courtesy Vancouver Natural History Society

RECOMMENDED READING

There are many excellent books on the market, among the most useful and informative being the following:

The Audubon Society Guide to Attracting Birds. Stephen W. Kress. Charles Scribner's & Sons. 1985.

A Bibliography of British Columbia Ornithology. Volume 1. R. Wayne Campbell, Harry R. Carter, Christopher D. Shepard & Charles J. Guiguet. British Columbia Provincial Museum. 1979.

A Bibliography of British Columbia Ornithology, Volume 2. R. Wayne Campbell, Tracey D. Hooper & Neil K. Dawe. Royal British Columbia Museum. 1988.

The Bird Feeder Book. Donald and Lillian Stokes. Little Brown and Company. 1987.

The Birdfinding Guide to Canada. J. Cam Finlay. Hurtig Publishers. 1984.

The Birds of British Columbia. C. J. Guiguet. British Columbia Provincial Museum.
1 The Woodpeckers. 2 The Crows and their Allies. Handbook #6. 1954.
Alien Animals in British Columbia. Handbook #14. 1957.
Chickadees, Thrushes, Kinglets, Pipits, Waxwings and Shrikes. Handbook #22. 1964.
Diving Birds and Tube-nosed Swimmers. Handbook #29. 1971.
Gulls, Terns, Jaegers and Skua. Handbook #13. 1971.
The Owls. Handbook #18. 1970.
The Shorebirds. Handbook #8. 1962.
Upland Gamebirds. Handbook #10. 1970.
Waterfowl. Handbook #15. 1971.

Birds of British Columbia: Nonpasserines - Loons through Woodpeckers. R. Wayne Campbell, Neil K. Dawe, Ian McTaggart-Cowan, John M.Cooper, Gary W. Kaiser and Michael C. E. McNall. Royal British Columbia Museum, Victoria. Available late 1989.

Birds of Canada. Revised Edition. W. Earl Godfrey. National Museum of Natural Sciences. 1986.

Birds of North America: A Guide to Field Identification. Chandler S. Robbins, Bertel Bruun & Herbert S. Zim. Golden Press, Western Publishing Inc. 1983.

Complete Book of Birdhouse Construction for Woodworkers. Scott D. Campbell. Dover Publications, Inc. 1984.

Field Guide to the Birds of North America. S. L. Scott (editor). National Geographic Society. 1983.

Field Guide to Western Birds. R. T. Peterson. Houghton Mifflin. New Edition: 1989.

Trees, Shrubs and Flowers to Know in British Columbia. C. P. Lyons. J. M. Dent & Sons (Canada) Limited. 1976.

Vancouver Birds in 1971. R. Wayne Campbell, Michael G. Shepard and Wayne C. Weber. Vancouver Natural History Society. 1972.

Vancouver Birds in 1972. R. Wayne Campbell, Michael G. Shepard and Bruce A. Macdonald. Vancouver Natural History Society. 1974.

Where to Find Birds in British Columbia. Second edition. David M. Mark. Kestrel Press. 1984.

DIRECTORY OF ORGANIZATIONS

The Federation of B.C.
Naturalists
#321, 1367 West Broadway
Vancouver, B.C. V6H 4A9
phone 737-3057
fax 738-7175

Alouette Field Naturalists
#301, 9143 Saturna
Burnaby, B.C. V3J 7K1

Bowen Nature Club
Box 20, Site G, R.R.#1
Bowen Island, B.C. V0N 1G0

Langley Field Naturalists
Box 3234
Langley, B.C. V3A 4R6
Eunice Wilson 581-1274

Royal City Field Naturalists
844 Kent Street
New Westminster, B.C.
V3L 4W6

Sechelt Marsh
Protective Society
Box 543
Sechelt, B.C. V0N 3A0

Squamish Estuary
Conservation Society
Box 1274
Squamish, B.C. V0N 3G0

Vancouver Natural
History Society
Box 3021
Vancouver, B.C. V6B 3X5

White Rock and Surrey
Naturalists
Box 44
White Rock, B.C. V4B 4Z7

INDEX TO BIRDS

ABOUT THE AUTHORS

Robin Bovey is a writer and photographer living in western Canada. He worked for a variety of environmental agencies in Britain before moving to Canada. In 1988, he co-authored and did the photography for *Mosses Lichens and Ferns of Northwest North America*. He is the author of *Birds of Edmonton* and *Birds of Calgary* and is a keen birdwatcher.

R. Wayne Campbell has written more than 300 scientific and popular articles on the birds and other vertebrates of British Columbia. He is the lead author of *Birds of British Columbia* (Volume I, 1989), which is an analysis of over a million specimen, sight and breeding records of birds in the province. He is an Elected and Life Member of the American Ornithologists' Union and is a Registered Professional Biologist.

ABOUT THE ILLUSTRATORS

Lead illustrator Ewa Pluciennik, who specializes in water colour and oil paintings, was born and raised in Opole, Silesia, Poland where she received her artistic training. She has been living in Canada for nearly five years.

Contributing illustrators Kitty Ho and Donna McKinnon are freelance artists living in Alberta. Joan Johnston lives in British Columbia.